T

SALINE & BLAIRINGONE CHURCH

Pennies for Heaven

IAN COFFEY

KINGSWAY PUBLICATIONS
EASTBOURNE

ISBN 0 86065 257 2

Biblical quotations are from the New International Version,
© New York International Bible Society 1978.

The statistics on page 14 are
taken from the Central Statistical Office,
Economic Trends, September 1983.

Printed in Great Britain for
KINGSWAY PUBLICATIONS LTD
Lottbridge Drove, Eastbourne, E. Sussex BN23 6NT by
Richard Clay (The Chaucer Press) Ltd, Bungay, Suffolk
Typeset by Nuprint Services Ltd, Harpenden, Herts.

Contents

Foreword

Books on giving are not as popular as those on some
other topics. In Britain we tend to stay off the subject.
It is rarely preached about, and little instruction is
given to young people about it. The impression is
sometimes given that to speak in concrete terms
about giving is not very spiritual. How totally
unscriptural are such ideas! Neither in the Old
Testament nor in the New is the subject avoided.
The apostle Paul certainly had no inhibitions about
giving. He organized a collection for the material
support of the poorer members of the Jerusalem
church. Furthermore he told the Corinthians their
giving was to be both regular and related to income.

It is good to find a young man writing on this
subject and doing so in such clear terms. Ian Coffey's
approach is both scriptural and relevant. He traces
the subject of giving right through the Bible and
proceeds to give examples from recent history of men
whose material needs God met and who themselves
were generous givers.

This is an intensely practical book. Ian Coffey
earths the subject on which he writes and shows ways

in which Christians can most effectively give to the support of God's work in the world. Some will find what he has to say comes 'rather near the bone' and in that sense it is a disturbing book, but many of us need to be disturbed. Giving in British churches is generally speaking at a very low level. Ian is a son of the Manse and both he and his brother David are full-time Christian workers. He does not have an axe to grind but he does know from personal experience some of the fruits of meanness on the part of the Lord's people. There is, however, no trace of rancour or bitterness in what he has written, but rather a simple, straightforward and utterly scriptural plea for generous and even sacrificial giving by Christians. This book deserves to be widely read and taken seriously by all who acknowledge Jesus not only as Saviour but as Lord of their lives.

GILBERT KIRBY

Preface

I have always considered a list of 'thank you's' at the beginning of a book to be tedious and unnecessary. At least, I used to think that way until I began to write this book and realized how much I owed to the advice and help of friends in the writing of it.

This book is not just about a subject—it is more to do with a burden, which the dictionary defines as 'a load that is carried'. I must record my indebtedness to a number of Christian friends around the world whose insights have taught me much about giving and discipleship.

Clive Calver is heavily responsible for this book ever seeing the light of day, and I am grateful to him for being one of God's initiators. Two members of my church have been responsible for typing and retyping the manuscript—Mrs Ruth Adey, who helped in the early stages, and Sue Bonner who has borne the brunt of the work. I would particularly thank Sue, who fitted it all in with her busy life with consistent cheerfulness.

I would express my thanks to the Rev. Stephen Brady for his scholarly criticisms and Paul Bateman and Michael Beardsmore who, as financial experts, have added their own distinctive touches.

I work in a unique situation in that I am shared between a local church and a missionary society. My colleagues in the pastoral team and the members of Earls Hall Baptist Church, Southend, have taught me valuable lessons about giving, and I will always be grateful to the Lord for allowing me to walk part of my journey with them. The practical lessons in this book stem largely from our experience as a church as we have sought to be the people God wants us to be. We have not arrived—but at least we are moving.

My good friend and colleague, Dave Pope, has, as always, been a steady and wise counsellor and the Saltmine Trust is a 'family' whose love and commitment mean a great deal.

Lastly, and most important of all, I would like to express gratitude to my wife, Ruth, who is my most honest critic and faithful encourager. C. T. Studd's words to his fiancée, quoted later (p.102), sum up her influence on my life so well. My thanks to her and our family for their willingness to sacrifice our time together in order that this book could be written.

IAN COFFEY

1
God in the Cupboard

London's Albert Hall was packed to capacity. The audience was mainly under the age of forty. Their voices were raised in singing; faces were aglow with worship and praise to God as all across the audit-orium hands were raised high in the air and the words of the hymn thundered in repetition:

> Our God reigns! Our God reigns!
> Our God reigns! Our God reigns!

To hear them, to be with them, you had little doubt that he did.

Some months later the scene was the same although the people were different. The Albert Hall once again was packed. The audience was mixed in age and near to the orchestra a lively, colourful crowd lustily sang, clapped, cheered and shouted. Their singing was exuberant and as the orchestra swelled the sound of the words rang out:

> Rule Britannia, Britannia rule the waves
> Britain never, never, never shall be slaves!

The first of the occasions I have described was a Christian meeting, a gathering of believers from churches of all denominations across the country. Their singing was worship directed towards the God of heaven. Their declaration was emphatic: in this tottering, decaying world God was in control. His plans were being worked out in human history. The song was also for many people a declaration of personal allegiance: 'God reigns in this world and he reigns in my life.'

The second occasion was, of course, the traditional last night of the Proms, the final evening in a series of concerts held annually in London. It is customary that the audience join the orchestra in the patriotic song *Rule Britannia*. Britannia never existed as a real person. She is a legendary lady dressed in a robe and helmet who carries a large trident. She personifies the British nation and the song refers to the great days of the Empire when the British navy ruled the seaways of the world. The song is certainly stirring, but it is also a little sickening when you compare statistics with the lyrics. 'Britain never, never, never shall be slaves...' is a bit hollow in a nation where £1,832 million is spent annually on gambling; £5,882 million on tobacco and £12,275 million on alcohol.

What disturbs me about the two scenes I have just described is that for some professing Christians the God who reigns is about as relevant as Britannia with her trident. Part of the reason for the spiritual bankruptcy in the church in Britain is that for years we have sung one thing and believed another. We have claimed to be 'all one in Christ Jesus' (Gal 3:28) in our conventions but have gladly ducked behind our denominational battlements for the other fifty-one weeks of the year. We have shouted at the world that the good news of Jesus that we preach liberates and fulfils men and yet our lives fail to demonstrate the product. We claim to believe in a prayer-answering God and yet our prayers are so infrequent and self-centred the world sees little of the supernatural about the church. This book attempts to take up and examine one small part of what it should mean when God reigns in a human life. The Lord Jesus Christ repeatedly spelt out the terms on which people entered his discipleship school:

> If anyone would come after me, he must deny himself and take up his cross daily and follow me. For whoever wants to save his life will lose it, but whoever loses his life for me will save it (Lk 9:23–24).

Problems come for some people in their Christian lives because they have not really seen who the Lord Jesus Christ is. They have perhaps understood that he came to be the Saviour who paid the debt and penalty for sin at Calvary. They may even acknowledge his authority and power as demonstrated in the Resurrection, but their understanding falls short. Jesus Christ comes to an individual life as the King of all kings. He brings forgiveness and deliverance but these are only part of his purpose in saving people. His work is to reconcile, or bring back, people to the God who made them (2 Cor 5:18 and Rom 5:10). A Christian is someone who, by God's grace, has been born again into God's family, a person who exercises faith in Jesus Christ as Saviour *and Lord*. It is the aspect of lordship that is forgotten and neglected by some who preach the gospel, and that is why there are professing Christians in our nation today who know little of the kingship of Christ in their lives.

Some time ago I met a missionary who had just returned from Thailand. He talked of his work with the people in that country and how he had spent hours in their homes speaking about Jesus. In most Thai homes, he said, there is a 'god shelf' in a prominent place. Here a collection of idols would stand, together with candles and assorted religious bric-a-brac. This would be the focus of attention for part of each day as the family would pray and beseech the gods to favour them. We may be tempted to smile condescendingly on such heathen customs and be glad that missionaries take the gospel to pagan societies. In fact, Thai society is no more pagan than our own. The spiritual darkness of Britain is great and so is the ignorance of many of us who would call ourselves God's people in this land. We may not have a 'god shelf' in the living-room, but we certainly have a picture of God in a cupboard. He is kept there for emergencies. He is always on hand to help in the crises and decisions of our lives. He is readily available to dole out blessings beneficently as if they were jelly babies. God has become the good-guy-next-door who rushes to my aid at the sound of a whistle. If that sounds blasphemous to you—it is! That is the picture of God that some people have and it is a denial of all that he really is. Scripture speaks of him enthroned in splendour and majesty, surrounded in heaven by a praising chorus of thousands upon thousands of angelic beings. Compare Daniel's vision of the eternal, holy God with the distorted cartoon version we have made him to be:

> As I looked, thrones were set in place, and the Ancient of Days took his seat.
> His clothing was as white as snow;
> the hair of his head was white like wool.
> His throne was flaming with fire, and its wheels were all ablaze.
> A river of fire was flowing, coming out from before him.
> Thousands upon thousands attended him; ten thousand times ten thousand stood before him.
> The court was seated, and the books were opened (Dan 7:9–10).

Daniel saw God in his majesty, holiness and splendour. He also saw him as the ultimate authority. The One before whom all men, one day, would be accountable for their actions, words and thoughts.

A national newspaper recently carried an account of a church that was offering a free plastic glow-in-the-dark Jesus to anyone who wrote to them. Many people today are worshipping idols. Some of God's people are worshipping a plastic, glow-in-the-dark Jesus and not the living Lord of glory that he truly is.

In case you're wondering if this is a book about Christian giving, let me assure you that it is. But because our understanding of God and his gospel is defective our Christian lifestyle is often far removed from the standards of the New Testament. The level of Christian giving in our country is appalling. Church buildings are decaying; Christian workers are badly underpaid; missionary societies cut back on their programmes because of severe lack of support. Lack of response when it comes to Christian giving is only a symptom. The disease is serious; it is called 'a wrong view of God'. When we see God for who he is, and acknowledge Jesus Christ as *the King*, then our giving flows from that fundamental relationship. God is no longer my servant, but I am his steward.

For a long time the topic of money has been a taboo subject among evangelical Christians. A man can preach on almost any matter but if he preaches on money he is condemned as unbalanced and dismissed as having some mercenary motive of his own. Just as sex was forbidden territory in the hushed confines of Victorian society, so today the church draws up her skirts in horror at the mention of cash. Why are we so sensitive? Possibly because the preacher that mentions Christian giving is touching on a very raw nerve. The Holy Spirit has a habit of doing that, not merely to cause pain but to produce healing. God has been saying much for many years to the British church on the subject of giving, but we have failed time and time again to listen—and act! Tom Rees, an evangelist greatly used by God during his lifetime, wrote a booklet well over twenty years ago on the subject of giving. He drew the comparison between the attitude of American Christians and their British counterparts on the issue of giving to God's work. Tom Rees said that, in the USA, irrespective of higher living standards, the Christian church was realistic in its giving, and it didn't consistently brush the subject under the carpet. He added these prophetic words:

I fear that if we do not follow the example of our American brethren in obeying the Word of God in the matter of giving, the witness of the Evangelical British Church will wither sadly (Tom Rees, *Money Talks*, distributed by Hildenborough Hall, p.18).

What is the cause of this disease that seems to have gripped us? I believe there are a number of contributory factors:

1. Our vision of God is inadequate

As we have already seen, if we view God as a king then we shall treat him as such. If we view him as the good-guy-next-door then we will only pass on to him the dog-ends of our earnings. Here lies the heart of the problem as we view the need of the church in Britain—we have made God in our own image and worshipped a plastic twentieth-century idol we call 'God' but is as lifeless as the Golden Calf made by Aaron and the Children of Israel (Ex 32). We need the Holy Spirit to give us a vision of God as God—revealed in Scripture, seen as a man in Jesus, active and sovereign in history. We must repent of our wrong view of God, by which we have dishonoured him and hindered his will in our lives.

2. Our understanding of Scripture is inaccurate

Scripture is packed full of teaching on the subject of the people of God and their possessions. The startling attitude of the early church in the matter of money and goods shook the world of its day. Church historians sometimes refer to the church in Acts as 'the primitive church'. When you compare their lifestyle with ours you can be forgiven for thinking 'who is calling who *primitive*?' Like it or not, we have ignored pages of God's revelation to man on the subject of our responsibility over possessions entrusted to us by God. If you think that is a sweeping statement, start to write down on a piece of paper each reference in the Bible to money, possessions, stewardship or God's authority over a person's whole life. Then think back to the last sermon you heard on principles of Christian giving. We may pride ourselves in being 'people of the Book' with a heritage of biblical understanding, but our behaviour betrays our lack of a real grasp of the Scriptures.

3. Our commitment to the body of Christ is insufficient

The teaching of the New Testament dealing with Christians and their attitude to fellow believers can be summed up in the succinct challenge of Paul to the church at Philippi: 'Each of you should look not only to your own interests, but also to the interests of others' (Phil 2:4).

Mutual care and concern for one another has been one of the exciting things many Christians have been rediscovering in recent years. The Holy Spirit has been showing us how the love of God 'shed abroad in our hearts' is not just an academic truth but must overflow in practical demonstrations of commitment to others in the body of Christ. It is because we have lost sight of what the body of Christ is meant to be that

our understanding of financial help and support has
been defective. When you view the church as a limited
company or a social centre on a level with the golf
club, your approach to financial giving will be
governed by a subscription outlook. If you see the
church as God describes it, the body of Christ on
earth, with each member dependent on the others,
then the question of giving becomes an act of love
rather than a task of duty. It is an offence to God that
communities of Christians live comfortable lives
while their pastors rely on the state to supplement
their income. It dishonours and grieves God that
missionaries on the field have their allowances cut or
held up because of the failure of local churches to see
the biblical concept of sending people out in the work
of spreading the gospel. It is a denial of the gospel
when some members of a church fellowship live in
severe financial need while other members have more
than enough to live comfortably. The world fails to
believe in God's alternative society because so often
we fail to demonstrate the radical difference Jesus
makes. When we begin to understand and live out
the truth of the church being the body of Christ then
it follows that: 'If one part suffers, every part suffers
with it; if one part is honoured, every part rejoices
with it' (1 Cor 12:26).

4. Our dedication to world evangelism is ineffective

If most professing Christians were faced with the
question: 'Do you want others all across the world to
come to know Jesus?' there would be little doubt

21

about the automatic answer that would roll off our tongues. Any preacher throwing that question out at the average convention would get 100% response to his appeal! Why then do our actions demonstrate the opposite to our words? Why are so few prepared to go wherever God calls them, to leave behind the comfort of a cosy Christian life and to get out to the front-line of the battle? Why are so many faithful and spiritually adventurous women having to take the role of men across the world? Dr Helen Roseveare is a medical missionary who served God in Africa for many years and suffered brutality and imprisonment for the sake of Jesus Christ. She makes this telling observation concerning British Christians and our lack of commitment to the advancing of Christ's kingdom:

Some university meetings are packed out. One I spoke at, only forty attended five years ago. This time there were over three hundred and eighty. People are coming. They are intrigued. They are interested. They are ready to be challenged. They ask marvellous questions. I get thrilled! And what then? We never see them again. Missionary societies are crying out for candidates. Where do they go? What happens? Apathy comes in. They are caught up in materialism. They are caught up in the new creed of the West—'What do I get out of it?' I go to speak at 'Career Classes' and when I start to talk I wonder why they look so puzzled. And I have forgotten that I happen to be a doctor and they thought I was going to talk on medicine as a career. I know of only one career—that's being a missionary for the Lord Jesus Christ, so I give them all I've got. And then I ask them for questions and every time within the first three questions someone will come up with this, 'What do I get out of it?' 'Is there a pension?' 'What is the salary?' 'Who pays my children's fees in the future?', etc. They are brainwashed with it. They must get a secure job, not be redundant. They must know at the end there is a pension coming. They like the perks, 'Has the job got a car with it or a house?' And it's seeped right through the church (*Dedication Magazine*, September 1980).

Even if God doesn't call you to serve him as a full-time missionary, he has called you to give to and support evangelism throughout the world. If a lack of commitment to world evangelism has paralysed our *going* to tell others the good news about Jesus, it has certainly affected our *giving*. In the realm of supporting the spreading of the gospel never has so much been left by so many to so few.

5. Our attitude towards possessions is incorrect

Western society is possession crazy. In a world where two-thirds of the population live in poverty, materialism is a sin. The advertisers pulverize the consumer from the hoardings, through the glossy magazines and across the television screen. It is all too easy for the Christian to become squeezed into the world's mould. We are made to believe as members of the consumer society that life would simply be incomplete without that latest piece of electronic gadgetry. Some Christians see God as more of a shareholder in their lives rather than the sole owner. That is not, however, the view of the Bible. Redemption is one of the keys to understanding the message of the New

Testament. Behind the use of the word there are the ideas of paying a market price for a slave or meeting a ransom demand for a prisoner. (There are three Greek words used in the New Testament meaning 'to redeem': *agorazo*; *exagorazo*; *lutroo*. Each word has the sense of 'buying back', which is what God has done for us in Christ.)

This idea is taken up and applied by New Testament writers as meaning that the follower of Jesus Christ no longer has rights over himself or his possessions—'you were bought at a price. Therefore honour God with your body' (1 Cor 6:20). The Bible gives no justification to the view that God is only interested in our souls. Our spiritual salvation and well-being is of paramount concern to God, but the lordship of Christ must extend over all aspects of our lives, including our possessions.

We are stewards of God's property. The health and strength to work, the privilege of employment and the gift of life itself all come from the hand of God. The money and material possessions that I gain are not mine, they are his. They are given to me on trust as a caretaker, and I am responsible for the way they are used. My house, furniture, car, clothes—in fact everything—belong to God. He is not my shareholder, I am his slave.

If that sounds far-fetched or extreme then I would point you back to the Bible and ask you, after prayer and study, what other conclusion could we possibly reach? In a materialistic age, one of the ways Christian people are called to demonstrate the radical change Jesus Christ makes is to practise faithfully and consistently the principles the word of God lays down concerning Christian stewardship.

I once went to speak at a senior school in the West Country. Before we went in to the assembly hall the headmaster stopped suddenly as we were leaving his study. 'Will you pray at the end or do you want me to say one?' he inquired. I assured him that it would be no problem for me to close the assembly with prayer. 'Are you sure?' he pressed, 'It's no problem; I can get one out of the cupboard!' He opened his cabinet to reveal prayers for every occasion neatly filed and indexed.

Is God filed away neatly in my cupboard, or is he on his throne? Read the Bible from Genesis to Revelation and you will find no support for fire-alarm faith. God is not a convenient commodity but a king. And it is when we acknowledge his kingship and authority that our Christian lives take on a New Testament shape.

If you have a 'God in the cupboard' vision, your attitude to giving will be worldly. You will assess your weekly church offering on the current going rate for a cinema seat, or less. You will be deeply offended when preachers or missionaries talk about tithing or the financial needs of Christian work. You will probably find it hard to handle the pastor buying a new suit or a Christian worker driving a new car. You will probably get hot and bothered at the mention of missionaries' needs or the challenge of the Third World. You will view others who give liberally as either spiritual show-offs or unbalanced extremists.

If your God really does reign on his throne and in your life you will be characterized not by 'how much does God want?' but 'how much can I give?' You will be prayerfully giving and constantly re-evaluating how the money you have been entrusted with should be used. You will rejoice when you see fellow believers being supported and cared for in a realistic way *and* you will be constantly open to God to direct your use of money and possessions for his glory.

What sort of vision of God do you have? Is he on the throne or in a cupboard?

2

Foundations

Stepping into the pages of the Bible is like taking an action-packed tour around a fascinating country. The landscape is vast. We come across places where God has acted and people that he has used. There is enough to grip your attention for a lifetime—and more! In addition to recording people that God has used and places where God has acted, the Bible shows us *principles* that God has given. The Bible is, in every sense, a Christian's guidebook to life. The Bible as God's Book of Truth reveals to us *God*. The Bible tells us of God's plan of salvation through the Lord Jesus Christ, and also spells out how saved people should live. Although we have an Old Testament and a New Testament, they both make up one Bible. Neither is complete without the other. As far as the Old Testament is concerned, we may have fallen into the trap of thinking that as God caused it to be written by the Jews, for the Jews, then we should leave the Jews to it! In fact, it is of great importance in giving us foundations in our understanding and worship of the living God. When we come to look closely at the Old Testament, we find that giving to God is part of man's duty if he really wants to worship God properly. As we look at the rolling landscape of the Old Testament we shall home in on some individuals who illustrate the foundations that God has given us concerning giving and worship.

'From the beginning...'

Long before God gave his law through Moses at Mount Sinai, he had revealed something of himself to men. In his dealings with men such as Adam, Abraham and Jacob, although they had no Bible or written documents on which to base their faith, God conveyed to them deep truths about himself and the standards he expected from those who claimed to be worshippers of him. We are going to look at three incidents that occurred hundreds of years before the law of God was given through Moses. These examples show us that from the very beginning of God's dealings with men, giving is an essential part of worship and a life of commitment.

For our first example, we need to go back to the first harvest festival service ever held (Gen 4:2–12). Cain and Abel were the sons of Adam and Eve and they each brought an offering to God. Cain, who was a farmer, brought an offering of fruit and vegetables. Abel worked as a shepherd and his gift for God came from his flock. He brought the best animals to be given as a sacrifice. Although the Bible is silent on this point, we must assume that God had revealed to men that such offering should be brought as tokens of gratitude towards God. When we ask the question

'Why did Cain and Abel give?' we deduce that they were acknowledging the kingship of God and his authority over everyone and everything. Cain and Abel were acting out of their belief that they were merely caretakers of all that God had entrusted to them. We can learn much from the Hebrew word used in this passage and translated in English as 'offering'. The same word was used in human affairs of a gift given in homage or allegiance to a king or ruler. By bringing gifts that were part of their every-day life—fruit, vegetables and animals—Cain and Abel were demonstrating in a practical way that they were worshippers of the living God.

If we study this incident of Cain and Abel's offer-ings, the tragic aftermath of murder and then look across at the explanation of the story in the New Testament letter to the Hebrews, we find an impor-tant truth (Heb 11:4). God looked beyond the gifts and into the hearts of the givers. Cain's offering (fruit and vegetables) was not accepted by God. Perhaps Cain brought his gift with excessive pride in his own ability as a farmer; possibly he felt jealous as he looked over his shoulder to see what his brother was bringing; perhaps he brought his own gift grudgingly and with no real sense of gratitude to God in his heart. By contrast, Abel's hand was in tune with his heart and he received the commendation from God that comes to everyone who marries their beliefs and their behaviour.

Travelling further into the biblical landscape, we come, some generations later, to one of the greatest men in the Old Testament, Abraham. He is seen as the father of the Jewish faith, because the history of the nation of Israel begins with him. When we read the New Testament we find that he is described as spiritual forefather of 'all who believe' (Gal 3:7). This makes his life one of special significance when we come to look at the way God blessed and used him. This forefather and forerunner demonstrates for us what faith is. The man who is described as the friend of God teaches us, from his examples of failure and success, how to live a life of faith.

One amazing incident from Abraham's colourful life follows a great victory God gave him against four hostile kings and their armies (Gen 14:17–24). With a mere 318 men, Abraham had rescued some of his family who had been captured by this vast military co-operative. As the victorious Abraham returned with his men, a king—who was also a priest—came out to meet him. The king/priest was named Melchizedek and he brought Abraham bread and wine and prayed that God's blessing would rest upon our great spiritual forefather.

In the New Testament we find a fascinating commentary on Melchizedek (Heb 7:1–28). This mysterious king/priest is a picture (or type) of the Lord Jesus Christ. Abraham's response to Melchizedek is to give him a tenth (or tithe) of the goods he has taken from the defeated kings and their armies. This is the first reference in the Bible to the practice of tithing, that is to say, the giving of a *tenth* (tithe) of all one owns to God. When we apply the question 'Why did Abraham give?', we discover that it was an act of gratitude for the help, love and blessing God had poured out on his life. Abraham recognized Melchizedek's greatness as a king and priest, and the gift of 10% of the goods he had taken was not a tribute to a man but a gift for God. For Abraham, worship had a practical meaning. We are not able to point to a verse in the Bible that commanded Abraham to tithe—and that makes this incident all the more amazing! In his relationship with God, Abraham had grasped the point that giving was a practical expression of his worship.

Next, we look at Jacob—another giant of the Old Testament. His name tells us a great deal about his character. 'Jacob' means 'he grasps the heel', and although this refers to the actual circumstances of his birth, it is also a graphic description of his outlook on life. Jacob grew up to be a deceiver and twister, until God got hold of him. The con-artist was fashioned into something beautiful and usable by the hand of God. As part of that great changing process, God appeared to Jacob one night as he lay sleeping, an exhausted runaway (Gen 25:10–22). God repeated to Jacob the mind-blowing promises he had first given to his grandfather Abraham and then to his father, Isaac. He promised Jacob that he would protect and watch over him all his life. When Jacob woke, he built a monument and called the place where he slept 'Bethel', which means house of God, as a permanent reminder of God's promise to him. He then made a solemn vow. He promised that if God was as good as his word, then he would build a place of worship at Bethel, and give God a tenth of any material goods he chose to bless Jacob with.

In case you are tempted to think this is just a slick Jewish businessman doing a deal with the Almighty for 10% of the action, provided blessings were round the corner, think again! Jacob was not bargaining with God, he was responding to him: 'All that you give me—be it much or little—one tenth will be given to you.' Why did Jacob promise to give? He made his solemn pledge as a response to God's love and faithfulness and as a demonstration of his commitment to being God's servant.

These opening chapters of the Bible show us that giving of material possessions is an important ingredient in the life of anyone who claims to be a dedicated servant and follower of God. These men were living hundreds of years before God gave his law through Moses. They were not following the codes and practices of a complicated religion, their faith was naked to say the least. At the very core of their commitment to the living God, they had an understanding that he deserved and desired worship more meaningful than hymns and handouts. Those who feared and loved him brought gifts from their own possessions as an acknowledgement of his supreme kingship over everything, as an act of worship, with thankfulness and love, and as a reminder that men are mere caretakers of all God has entrusted to them for a few short years.

The Maker's instructions

When God met Moses at Mount Sinai and gave to him the law, it was an important moment in history. Many Christians have failed to understand the place of God's law, and the importance that it plays in the good news concerning Jesus. Some have simply regarded Genesis to Malachi as totally unimportant for the Christian, foolishly thinking that because we call the Old Testament 'Old', it must be obsolete. Others have got so muddled up that they act as if Jesus had never come, for they live under the Old Covenant. Many of these 'kosher' Christians are so anchored to the law that one cannot help wondering why they are not consistent enough to hold meetings in tents and slaughter the occasional goat. Still others have opted for the middle path that acknowledges the importance of the law, but cannot really decide which bits are for today and which bits are not!

In order to grasp the New Testament teaching about the place and importance of the law, we need to see that the words of instruction God gave at Mount Sinai fall into three categories:

The ceremonial law   —   which is temporary
The judicial law   —   which is related to
                                   Israel as a nation
The moral law   —   which is permanent

Ceremonial law

This is detailed, and sets out how men can approach a holy God, how sacrifice for sin can be made, how the priesthood is to be chosen and maintained.

Judicial law

In judicial law God lays down rules of law and conduct governing life in the nation of Israel and a pattern of punishments and means of restitution when crimes have been committed.

The instructions concerning the worship of God

were temporary, waiting for the arrival of the greatest of all high priests, Jesus Christ. His sacrifice for sins would be powerful, once and for all. Goats and bulls are no longer needed. The regulations concerning life in Israel, although giving a pattern for our civil and criminal law, were specifically aimed at one nation at a specific time in history.

The moral law

The moral law, as revealed in the Ten Commandments, is as permanent as God himself. This came to the Israelites, and through them to the world, that all men might understand something of God's holiness and standards for living. Those who break God's law are guilty of sin and this is punishable by death. This law stands today, but Christ has come to set men free from the curse of lawbreaking, so that by his death we may be free from the legal demands of the law and cleansed from our sin of failing to keep it. Christ sets men free—free to serve God. When we ask the question 'How do I please God?', Christ points us to the law as God's expression of holiness. Instead of the 'Thou shalt nots' being a command that we fear, we find in Christ they become promises we can treasure. With Christ living as Lord of a person's life, the command that killed becomes a promise that liberates. When Jesus is Lord 'thou *shalt* not commit adultery' because he gives the grace that is needed to live a holy life.

We can learn much from the law about God, because it tells us about his own character. What the law lays down concerning worship is not binding because Christ has given us a New Covenant, but

34

what the law tells us is instructive if we want to live lives that please God.

What does God say through the law concerning giving? First of all he laid down tithing as an indispensable part of worship (Lev 27:30–33). A tenth of everything—grain, fruit or flocks—automatically belonged to God, 'it is holy to the Lord'. If, for any reason, a man needed to buy back his tithe, then he should add a fifth of its value to the price of the gift. God wanted his people to realize that everything they possessed ultimately came from God. The tithe would be a permanent and costly reminder that all that a man owned had *God* stamped upon it.

The second interesting point to notice is that God laid on his people the responsibility for the proper support of the priesthood (Num 18:15–32). The people were not left to give 'as the Lord leads', but their tithes were to support the priests who were full-time servants of God. The priests, in turn, were to tithe all that they received for the support of the High Priest. The nine-tenths that remained would be treated as their wages for their work in the service of God. In this holy attitude of co-operation, God laid down the mutual care and responsibility that had to exist in the nation of Israel. The principle was clearly applied to people and priests: one-tenth of all a man earned belonged to God.

Thirdly, we discover that the gifts of the people to God were to be used to help the poor in the nation (Deut 26:12ff.). The alien ('refugee' could be a twentieth-century translation of this word), the fatherless and the widow are seen as people who must be cared for. The law lays down that it is a man's religious duty to help such needy people.

A fourth lesson we draw from the law is that tithing is the *minimum* required by God: 'Burnt offerings and sacrifices, your tithes and special gifts, and all the choice possessions you have vowed to the Lord' (Deut 12:11) gives us some indication of the extent of practical worship that was required of the nation of Israel. The tithe belonged to God and when that was given a man had done no more than the least of what was expected of him. Gifts and offerings began once the tithe had been apportioned! During each year, God ordained special feasts that would be times of celebration reminding Israel of God's gracious intervention in her history. Such feasts were to be times of remembering, rejoicing and *giving*. God gives clear instructions how the men of Israel were to appear before him: 'No man should appear before the Lord empty-handed: Each of you must bring a gift in proportion to the way the Lord your God has blessed you' (Deut 16:16–17).

The fifth thing to notice from the instructions of God given through the law is that giving is to be a delight rather than a drudge. God made provision for an annual party to be held in his honour, an occasion when a family could sit down and eat their tithe! (Deut 14:22–26.) This was to be a time of happiness and rejoicing, as everyone was reminded of God's goodness to them.

From this brief survey, we can clearly see that worship for the people of God in the Old Testament was to be no empty-handed thing. Giving was a fundamental part of Israelite religion. Worship was then, and should be now, a costly business.

Robbery, repentance and revival

As we continue to gaze at the Old Testament landscape, we discover that many aspects of the history of Israel were disastrous. Again and again, Israel rebelled against God at every point of the law. They ignored his messengers, the prophets, and deliberately went the way of 'doing their own thing'. At such low times in the nation's history there were quite genuine spiritual revivals. When we study these times of revival closely we find that the restoration of the practice of bringing tithes and offerings is apparent on almost every occasion. God's powerful messengers, the prophets, brought strong words to the nation at various stages of her history. They, unlike many modern-day preachers, were not frightened to touch on uncomfortable subjects such as giving.

When King Hezekiah came to the throne, the worship of God had fallen into an appalling state. The temple had been shut, the priests had neglected their duties and the people no longer remembered God's great acts in history. Even the great feast of the Passover had been neglected by many. Hezekiah restored the situation in a diligent reformation, to which the nation and priesthood responded. In this time of spiritual renewal we read:

> The King contributed from his own possessions for the morning and evening burnt offerings and for the burnt offerings on the Sabbaths, New Moons and appointed feasts as written in the Law of the Lord. He ordered the people living in Jerusalem to give the portion due to the

priests and Levites so that they could devote themselves to the Law of the Lord. As soon as the order went
out, the Israelites generously gave the first fruits of their
grain, new wine, oil and honey and all that the fields
produced. They brought a great amount, a tithe of
everything.... When Hezekiah and his officials came
and saw... they praised the Lord and blessed his people
Israel (2 Chron 31:3–8).

Repentance is always a practical and costly thing.
The return of Israel to the ways of God meant a
recovering of God's pattern of giving.

By the time Hezekiah's great-grandson King
Josiah came to the throne, the religious state of Israel
was once again at a low ebb (2 Chron 34, 35). Josiah,
although a teenager, earnestly began to seek God for
his blessing on the nation. He began a thorough,
spiritual clean-up. Part of this involved much needed
repair work on the temple, which had been allowed
to deteriorate. He arranged an appeal fund of the
people's gifts to be used for the purpose of repairing
this important building. The money was used wisely
and well for the temple to be repaired, and during the
course of the work part of the law of Moses was
discovered. Not for the last time, God's word had got
lost in a church! This led to a serious study of God's
instructions to Moses and then followed a period of
heartfelt repentance led by King Josiah and the
leading men of the nation, and a putting right of the
many things that grieved God. With this book of the
law in their hands, Josiah and his senior men sought
to bring the nation back to the ways of God. All this
began when a God-fearing king stirred the people up
to give for the practical upkeep of a building. God's

ways are a lot more down-to-earth than some of us have ever imagined!

Moving on in Israel's history several decades, we find the disobedient people of God taken away into captivity by the Babylonian nation. Despite warnings given through the prophets, the nation had not returned with whole hearts to God. At times, as in the reigns of Hezekiah and Josiah, there had been those who had earnestly sought to go God's way, but the nation—both north and south—had failed to be the people God wanted them to be.

Following years of exile, God sent a small remnant back to the devastated Jerusalem. The city was a heap of rubble and the people leaderless and overwhelmed. God, as he always does, had a man for the moment—Nehemiah. This unique servant of God became the best bricklayer the world has ever seen! His task from God was twofold. First, to see the city of Jerusalem rebuilt; second, to see the religion of the nation re-established. In this second task he was not alone, but was given the able assistance of the priest, Ezra. The building work on Jerusalem was organized in an extraordinary way and, despite opposition, the walls were completed in the record time of fifty-two days! When the people assembled together, Ezra read out publicly the book of the law of Moses. This led to a remarkable open-air repentance service, where the people pledged themselves again to God's holy covenant. In that pledge, they committed themselves to begin again to bring tithes and offerings to the Lord. They assumed once more the responsibility of supporting the priesthood. These solemn promises were put in writing and the document was signed, on behalf of all of the people, by the leaders and priests. The final sentence of this binding agreement rang out: 'We will not neglect the house of our God' (Neh 10:39).

We are perhaps able to understand something of the grief in God's heart at the fickleness of human nature, when we discover, just a few chapters later, that the people soon returned to their old ways. Nehemiah returned to the King of Babylon to make a report on the return of Israel to their homeland. On his return he was horrified to discover the backsliding that had taken place.

> I also learned that the portions assigned to the Levites had not been given to them, and that all the Levites and singers responsible for the service had gone back to their own fields. So I rebuked the officials and asked them, 'Why is the house of God neglected?' (Neh 13:10–11).

Nehemiah sought, once again, to bring the people back to a lifestyle that matched their profession to be followers of the living God. Revival, renewal and reformation involve people in the expensive business of getting back to God's ways.

As we draw to a close on this brief look at the Old Testament, we must not move on without referring to God's army of messengers, the prophets. Two of them in particular brought strong challenges on the subject of finance.

Haggai had a burden to see the ruined temple at Jerusalem rebuilt. He had returned with the exiles from Babylon and had seen the miraculous rebuilding of the city. His concern was for the temple, the focal point of the people's worship. One writer has described Haggai as 'a goad for God' as he rebuked the people for falling behind with the rebuilding of the temple. The foundations of the building had been laid some years previously but apathy and discouragement set in and the work had come to a standstill. The people made many excuses—'The time is not yet right to get on with the work'—it sounded spiritual, but it was not! Haggai's word from God was strong: 'Is it a time for you yourselves to be living in your panelled houses, while this house remains a ruin?' (Hag 1:3).

God challenges the people to look to their own circumstances. He points out that they were not materially well off. Although much had been planted, the harvest that resulted was meagre. Haggai then delivers God's solution—'Get on and build!' God promises to bless his people richly when they get their priorities right. If they are prepared to 'seek first God's kingdom' then they will be in line to experience his blessing and reward.

The second prophet gives us the last book of the Old Testament, Malachi. He brought God's word some years after Haggai. The temple had been rebuilt, but the promised blessing of God had not yet come. Times were hard; famine, drought and ruined crops had been met by spiritual indifference on the part of God's people. Many questioned whether there was any point in serving God and obeying his commandments. Malachi, as God's spokesman, put a heart-searching question:

'A son honours his father, and a servant his master. If I am a father, where is the honour due to me? If I am a master, where is the respect due to me?' says the Lord Almighty (Mal 1:6).

Among the many things that God has against his priests and people is the fact that they are guilty of daylight robbery.

Will a man rob God? Yet you rob me. But you ask, 'How do we rob you?' In tithes and offerings. You are under a curse—the whole nation of you—because you are robbing me (Mal 3:8–9).

The way a man gives to God is an expression of what his heart feels about God. The spiritual apathy prevalent here, as at many periods of Israel's history, had resulted in the failure to bring the tithes and offerings due to God. Notice that God takes this *personally*; they are not guilty of carelessness or neglect alone, but of robbing God. You can only rob someone when you take what rightly belongs to them. They were guilty not just of forgetting to 'give God something', but of taking and keeping for themselves what was due to him. Malachi spells out the way to put things right:

'Bring the whole tithe into the storehouse, that there may be food in my house. Test me in this,' says the Lord Almighty, 'and see if I will not throw open the floodgates of heaven and pour out so much blessing that you will not have room enough for it' (Mal 3:10).

In spite of the economic situation and escalating inflation, God tells his people to give sacrificially. He invites them to put him to the test, to go out on a limb, and see how much blessing he will pour upon them. When God speaks here of blessing he is not simply referring to spiritual joy, but his blessing would rest on their land with its fruit, crops and flocks. *Real* giving must be a sacrifice, but it is also a stepping stone to knowing God's blessing being poured out in the wonderful way that we read of in Malachi's prophecy. People through the centuries have taken up the challenge and promise of these verses in Malachi's prophecy. As we shall see later, it has never been recorded by anyone, anywhere, at any time, who has been obedient to this command and failed to see God fulfilling what he has promised. On the contrary, thousands upon thousands have learned the spiritual truth contained here—'Trust God—he is big enough!' When that trust is translated into sacrificial giving the blessing that rebounds on an individual life is inexpressible. God's promise, centuries old though it may be, is as true today as it was when first given.

There is one last passage of Scripture that we need to consider. This statement undergirds the whole concept of giving in the Old Testament. God never wanted his people to forget all he had done for them. He urged them never to forget his blessing and material provision and warned them against ever believing their own achievements had brought prosperity: 'But remember the Lord your God, for it is he who gives you the ability to produce wealth' (Deut 8:18). Israel was to give tithes, offerings and first-fruits as a permanent reminder that all they were and had came from God. Their worship was an act of allegiance and commitment to the living God—giving and holy behaviour were to be the overflow of their praise.

In case we feel tempted to view all this with detached interest, feeling that the relevance of God's dealings with Israel is not of concern to a twentieth-century Christian, read on!

Dr R. T. Kendall once told the following story to illustrate the relevance of fulfilling the law for the Christian believer:

There was once a man and woman who were unhappily married. The husband was a real dictator. He laid down certain ground rules by which their marriage would operate. He had no love for his wife, but demanded her absolute obedience to a list of rules he had written out. Through fear, his wife obeyed him. One day, the husband died—probably much to the relief of the hard-pressed wife! After a while she remarried. Her new husband was not a bit like her first husband; this man loved, respected and cared for her. For the first time in her life she knew the experience of being loved. One day, when clearing out an old dresser, she found the old rules from her first marriage. She read them through, and to her amazement found that she was actually fulfilling them in her second marriage without even realizing it. Because she was in love with her second husband, she was fulfilling all the demands of her previous self-centred spouse. What she had performed originally in fear she was now doing in freedom.

Dr Kendall concludes:

> When we fulfil the law of Christ on purpose, in love, the righteousness of the law is fulfilled accidentally.

Fear makes you give because you have to, love makes you give because you want to. It is important that, as Christians, we discover the difference, and then get on with the holy business of giving.

3
Agape = Action!

Most of us find the New Testament easier to read and understand than the Old Testament, as we often tend to think that Genesis to Malachi deals with history 'before God became a Christian', as one little boy delightfully put it! On the subject of money and possessions we may even fall into the trap of thinking that the New Testament does not have too much to say. We all run the risk of reading the Bible through our own cultural spectacles. The history of the Christian church is littered with examples of periods when vast chunks of Scripture were ignored or overlooked until God the Holy Spirit moved people to rediscover truth that had been lost or overlaid with man-made traditions. Even in the twentieth century we face that same danger. Uncomfortable passages of biblical truth that challenge and stir us to more radical discipleship are either glossed over or die the death of a thousand theological definitions. The New Testament has a great deal to say about the money that we earn and the way that we use it. Our need today as disciples of Jesus Christ is not to skirt around the more uncomfortable pages of God's truth by saying 'Is this culturally relevant?' The question we must ask ourselves is, 'Am I being biblically honest?'

To look closely at all that the New Testament has to say about money, possessions and how we use them is a vast exercise. One of the most profitable things for us to do would be to start to make a careful note of all the verses and passages that deal with this subject. In this chapter we are going to take a brief look at some of the main points on the subject that are made in the New Testament. We shall begin by looking at the Lord Jesus Christ himself, then at the first leaders of the church, and finally we shall look at the early Christian disciples.

The founder

Jesus is unique. Fully God and fully man he remains the only representative of God to men, and of men to God. It is his very uniqueness that makes his teaching so important. He is not just another messenger from God but in himself he *is* God. This means that by looking at his life and by listening to his teaching we discover what God thinks and feels about people and the way that we behave.

The way that he lived

Jesus, the King of kings, was not born in a royal palace but in a borrowed stable. Forget the Christmas-card image of a cosy nativity scene; it was like most stables, damp, dirty and smelly. He was not even born in a bed in the way that most babies arrive in this world, but was placed in a cattle-feeding trough. Mary and Joseph were poor people. When they came to offer the traditional sacrifice following the birth of Jesus they had to opt for the economy-version offering as they were too poor to afford the customary lamb (Lk 7:24; Lev 12:8). If early church tradition is reliable, Joseph died when Jesus was quite young, leaving him to be the breadwinner as the eldest in the family. He worked as a carpenter in the hill town of Nazareth. Far from being an easy life, Jesus did not enjoy economic security, but struggled as many of his countrymen did in a country dominated by a Roman army and the heavy taxation that went with it.

When Jesus began his public ministry at the age of thirty he called men to follow him. He and the disciples moved around the country in their itinerant ministry relying on the support and hospitality of their friends (Lk 8:3). They pooled their resources and made Judas the treasurer of the group (Jn 12:6) and, as well as using the funds to feed themselves, they distributed gifts to the poor (Jn 13:29). Throughout the three years of his public ministry Jesus had nowhere he could call home (Mt 8:20) and during the course of his ministry relied on the kindness of others. He borrowed a boat, he borrowed an ass, he borrowed a coin and he even borrowed the tomb he was buried in—although he only used it for a few days! When he came to the cross, he was stripped of the clothes that he wore and they were gambled over by the soldiers who crucified him. Jesus literally came into this world with nothing and left it with nothing. The God who created the universe and owned everything in it chose to live life on the breadline. Paul points to the example of Jesus' life when he said 'though he was rich, yet for your sakes he became poor, so that you through his poverty might become rich' (2 Cor 8:9). The sacrifice of Jesus on our behalf did not begin at Calvary, but at Bethlehem, and even further back than that in the heart of God.

The world into which Jesus was born was not that different from our own. Men have always associated power with wealth. Status has always depended on possessions. The world has always measured success by what a man *has* rather than what he *is*. Jesus chose to be a living contradiction of all those values, and he calls his followers to be the same. Some of his disciples were people of means (Mt 27:57; Lk 8:3), but they were people who *used* their means for the service of God, rather than just selfishly clinging onto them.

The things that he said

Jesus is the one supreme example of a teacher who practised what he preached. And he had quite a bit to say on the subject of money. He taught, and showed by his own example, that taxes should be paid whether they are levied by a religious or civil authority (Mt 17:24ff.; Mk 12:17). As always, Jesus denounced the hypocrisy of the Pharisees for the dutiful way in which they tithed even their spices, but yet left justice, mercy and faithfulness out of their everyday lives. Interestingly, Jesus tells them that they should have practised the latter without neglecting the former. Far from dismissing the Old Testament teaching on tithing, Jesus endorses it (Mt 23:23). Nowhere in his teaching do we find our Lord condemning the possession of private property. In the case of the rich young ruler, as we shall see later, he was putting his hand on a sensitive area of that man's life. (He still has that uncomfortable knack today.) In fact, the Bible as a whole does not teach that money in itself is evil, nor does it teach that possessions in themselves are bad. These things are neutral, neither good nor bad. It is the attitude we have towards them and the way that we use or abuse them that make the difference. However, Jesus clearly warned of the danger of making money into a god, and worshipping it:

> No-one can serve two masters. Either he will hate the one and love the other, or he will be devoted to the one and despise the other. *You cannot serve both God and Money* (Mt 6:24; italics mine).

The message is clear: you are either a slave to money or its master. A heart that loves God has no room for competitors. Jesus taught that a man should be more concerned with his spiritual savings account than with what he had invested with the building society: 'store up for yourselves treasures in heaven' (Mt 6:20). So many people cautiously put something by for 'that rainy day' and Jesus says 'Make sure you've got quite a bit put by for judgement day!' Jesus warned that wealth could be a great hindrance to someone entering God's kingdom (Lk 18:24f.) and that it could become an obstacle to your progress in his kingdom (Mk 4:19f.). One of his most powerful parables, the story of the rich fool, was told to bring home the point that a man's life does not consist of how much he owns; what really matters is how he stands before God. If ever there was a parable addressed to our generation today, then this is it (Lk 12:13–21).

Jesus taught his disciples that as kingdom people they should live out kingdom standards. In his kingdom manifesto, the sermon on the mount, he told them not to be preoccupied with worrying about what to eat, what to drink or what to wear. Although other people may hold the view that life revolves around these 'basics', kingdom people need to be concerned first and foremost with the kingdom: 'Your heavenly Father knows that you need [these things], but seek first his kingdom and his righteousness, and all these things will be given to you as well' (Mt 6:25ff.). As a practical object lesson concerning God's ability to provide for such everyday needs, Jesus sent his disciples out on a preaching tour with specific instructions to take nothing with them for the journey (Lk 9:3).

One of the most disturbing stories that Jesus told was about the rich man and Lazarus (Lk 16:19–31). It is disturbing for Western Christians who live among the privileged third of the world who have more than enough to eat while two-thirds go hungry. Lazarus was a poor beggar who lived at the gate of the rich man, who did nothing to help this broken, destitute man. Jesus said that the rich man died and went to hell not because he was wealthy but because he was indifferent. He had the power to help the beggar but did nothing.

This story, when seen in the light of one of Jesus' parables concerning the end of time, takes on an even more personal application. Jesus was illustrating the truth that one day God will write the final full stop on the page of human history. At that time all the nations will be gathered before the Lord Jesus Christ and men will be separated, just as the shepherd sorts out the sheep from the goats. The story is familiar: for some the separation will mean reward and for others it will mean punishment. But look again at the basis on which Jesus said men will be judged—*giving* (Mt 25:31ff.). Jesus was teaching quite clearly that the basis on which God will judge men is not merely beliefs but also their behaviour. 'I was hungry and you *gave* me food. I was thirsty and you *gave* me a drink. I was a stranger and you *gave* me hospitality. I needed clothes and you *gave* them to me. I was sick and you *gave* of yourself. I was in prison and you *gave* me your time.' Equally, those who refused help, who neglected to *give*, faced the righteous condemnation of the kingdom's King.

The words of Jesus never make for comfortable reading. They were never intended to. Dietrich Bonhoeffer said, 'When Christ calls a man, he bids him come and die.' Discipleship, in Jesus Christ's terms, spells death to self-interest. To claim to be his disciple while ignoring the practical implications of his lordship over our money and possessions and the way in which we use them, is to exchange genuine Christianity for a limp, lifeless cardboard replica of the real thing.

The people that he met

Jesus mixed with the rich and the poor. He showed that God is no respecter of persons, and that the universal sickness of sin knows no class barriers. Sick men, whatever their status, need a doctor. Jesus identified with the poor, having become one of them, and he preached good news to them, but in his ministry he did not ignore those who were materially better off.

Two men that Jesus met, both of whom were wealthy, provide an interesting contrast. One who remains anonymous is known as the 'rich young ruler' (Lk 18:23ff.). The second was a chief tax collector called Zacchaeus (Lk 19:1ff.). The rich young ruler could rightly be described as the man who had everything... but who went away with nothing. On the surface he had a lot going for him. He was wealthy, he had a position of status and he was a religious, righteous man. In spite of all this, there was an aching void in his life. Possessions had not brought spiritual satisfaction, and he came to Jesus with a simple but heartfelt question: 'What must I do to inherit eternal life?' Jesus, recognizing the young man's enthusiasm and sincerity, saw the real god in his life was money. He told him to sell everything he owned, freely distribute the proceeds to the poor and then he would discover the amazing freedom that slavery to Christ brings. This man of great wealth could not meet the bill, and so he sadly went away as empty and unfulfilled as he had come. It is interesting to see that Jesus let him go. Preaching on this passage, A.W. Tozer commented that most of us in that situation would have run after the young man and tried to negotiate with him. But Jesus spelt out the terms of discipleship in an uncompromising fashion. For the disciple of Christ there is room for only one master. You cannot serve God and money.

Some have read this passage in the New Testament and claimed that the only way you can become a true disciple is to sell everything that you own, but that is not what Jesus was teaching. One commentator on the New Testament has written:

When Jesus advised the rich young ruler to sell his possessions and give to the poor, he was not giving a general directive to all his followers, but specific advice to one whose great weakness was too great a love for riches (Donald Guthrie, *New Testament Theology*, IVP, p.943).

Another man with a similar problem was Zacchaeus. Luke tells us of his encounter with Jesus a short time after the rich young ruler had failed to meet the challenge of radical discipleship. Zacchaeus, far from having everything going for him, was a parasite. He was a chief tax collector for the prosperous city of Jericho. He made his living by extracting rich pickings from taxes he collected from his fellow countrymen on behalf of the Roman government. He was a traitor, a thief, a religious outcast and, to add to it all, his name meant 'the pure one'! When Jesus came into his life one dusty day on the Jericho High Street, an amazing change took place. He discovered that, in spite of the rottenness of his life, God actually knew him, cared about him and wanted to make something of him. There was no slick 'decisionism' about what happened to Zacchaeus that day. He came face to face with radical discipleship and he met the bill in full. He made an open, public declaration that he was a changed man. He pledged 50% of all that he owned to be given away to the poor, and he told the long list of his neighbours who had been swindled that they would receive back four times the amount that had been stolen. And Jesus did not specifically ask him to do any of that! It was his own immediate response to the love of Jesus. At the end of the day, Zacchaeus would have been left with the shirt on his back and not much more.

Not every disciple of Jesus had to empty his bank account before following him. We have already seen that Joseph of Arimathea and others were active in supporting Jesus' ministry. You do not have to be poor to be a disciple, but you do need to let Jesus have the right ownership over everything you possess. In the case of the rich young ruler, and Zacchaeus, Jesus spelt out what that right of ownership would mean. One man faced the challenge and discovered freedom, while the other ducked the issue and was left with frustration. The lordship of Jesus Christ in an individual's life means more than singing choruses and attending conferences. It involves acknowledging his right of ownership in every area of life, including the things that we own and the way in which we use them.

Another anonymous person that Jesus encountered during his earthly ministry was a poor widow who brought her offering to the temple (Mk 12:41ff.). Jesus was sitting and watching people as they brought their money to the temple treasury. It is an uncomfortable thought, but a serious one, that God still watches what happens when the offering plate comes round. Jesus was fully aware of the trumpet-blowing and showmanship that often accompanied such giving.

Indeed, he warned his disciples about this and encouraged them that secret and unpretentious giving was the sort that God desired (Mt 6:2ff.). He saw the wealthy give with a flourish, but he particularly noticed the poor, shuffling widow place her minute contribution to the treasury. He called his disciples' attention to her and used her as a living illustration of giving:

> I tell you the truth, this poor widow has put more in the treasury than all the others. They all gave out of their wealth; but she, out of her poverty, put in everything— all she had to live on.

God sees what we give—and also notices what is left behind. Jesus said that this widow demonstrated the sort of reckless faith that delights the heart of God. Others had given large amounts, but would hardly notice the dent in their income. She had given a small offering, but in proportion to what she owned it was a fortune. God never condemns extravagance when it comes to our giving to him. On the contrary, Jesus positively commended the faith and love that lay behind such a valuable offering.

The Lord Jesus Christ, through his life, by his teaching and in his encounters with people during his life on earth, demonstrated that submission to his lordship means that we give all that we are and all that we own to him. For a disciple, all property rights are signed over to the King. We remain but caretakers, responsible to him for the way in which our money and possessions are used.

Rudyard Kipling once addressed a group of

students about to graduate from university to make their fame and fortune in the world. He told them:

> As you go through life, don't seek for fame, or for money, or for power, because one day you will meet a Man who cares for none of these things, and then you will realize how poor you are.

Jesus was a living contradiction of all this world values. He calls us to be the same: to live out the principles of his alternative society, the kingdom of God. You may be poor, you may be rich, it matters not. What counts is that the King has total ownership of all that you possess.

The first Christian leaders

Giving as a part of the Christian life is interwoven as a theme throughout the New Testament. The leaders of the early Christian church, apostles such as Paul, Peter and John, demonstrated by their own lives of self-sacrifice, as well as through their teaching, that discipleship made uncompromising demands. It is worth looking at a few of the key points that are made in the New Testament epistles (or letters) on the subject of what we own and how we use it.

You are not your own

'You are not your own; you were bought at a price' (1 Cor 6:19, 20). Paul is writing on the subject of sexual immorality, but the principle he uses applies to every area of the Christian life. Paul has in mind the imagery of the slave market, an everyday picture in the experience of the first-century Christians. When a slave had been purchased by a master, he belonged exclusively to his new owner. He had no rights over his own life, because he now belonged to another. The ownership of Christ of a person's life was a basic concept for New Testament Christians. How shallow and unreal so much of our Western Christianity looks in the light of this sort of claim. David Watson writes:

> For countless Christians in the West, 'discipleship' means little more than going to church regularly, giving a proportion of one's income—usually at best one-tenth, and often far below that figure—and getting involved in a limited number of church activities (David Watson, *Discipleship*, Hodder & Stoughton, p.227).

The apostle's preaching was emphatic. 'Jesus Christ is Lord' was not just a creed but a whole way of living. This extends into every area of life and the sort of ethical problems and daily decisions that confronted their converts were to be faced in the light of the truth that they no longer belonged to themselves, but had been purchased by Christ.

Beware of wealth

It is not true to say that there are no wealthy members of the first Christian communities. But those who had been entrusted with riches were warned about the accompanying dangers and urged to be responsible stewards of what God had given them.

> For the love of money is a root of all kinds of evil. Some people, eager for money, have wandered from the faith and pierced themselves with many griefs (1 Tim 6:10).

58

Note that it is the *love* of money that is condemned here. Often this verse is misquoted as 'Money is the root of all evil.'

> Keep your lives free from the love of money and be content with what you have (Heb 13:5).

> Command those who are rich in this present world not to be arrogant nor to put their hope in wealth, which is so uncertain, but to put their hope in God, who richly provides us with everything for our enjoyment (1 Tim 6:17).

Fellowship means caring

Fellowship is a word which, among British Christians, has been devoid of meaning for many years. It has been relegated to mean little more than a weekly handshake and the offer of a cup of tea after a church service. One of the exciting things that the Spirit of God has been revealing in recent years to groups of Christians throughout our country is that *real* fellowship is a costly but precious thing. There are a group of words used in the New Testament, all related to the Greek work *koinonia*. It is a word that expresses a close and intimate relationship into which people enter. Outside of the New Testament, it was used in everyday Greek to refer to a business partnership, and even more intimately to describe the shared life that a married couple enter into. The nearest we can get to it in our language would be to call it 'sharingship', which does not make for good English, but it does make great Christianity! The writers of the New Testament letters constantly relate this 'sharingship' to taking a practical concern for the welfare of others around us.

He who has been stealing must steal no longer, but must work, doing something useful with his own hands, that he may have something to share with those in need Eph 4:28).

And do not forget to do good and to share [literally 'fellowship'] with others, for with such sacrifices God is pleased (Heb 13:16).

Command [the rich] to do good, to be rich in good deeds, and to be generous and willing to share (1 Tim 6:18).

Fellowship meant a costly giving of yourself to help and minister to the needs of others in the body of Christ. It became an outward demonstration to the world of the power of the gospel of Jesus Christ. He alone could transform self-centred individuals, divided by class and racial prejudice, to make them a committed group of people who shared and cared for one another. Ronald Sider writes:

For the early Christians *koinonia* was not the frilly 'fellowship' of church-sponsored bi-weekly outings. It was not tea, biscuits and sophisticated small talk in Fellowship Hall after the sermon. It was an unconditional sharing of their lives with the other members of Christ's body.
Christian fellowship meant unconditional availability to and unlimited liability for the other sisters and brothers emotionally, financially and spiritually (Ronald Sider, *Rich Christians in an Age of Hunger,* Hodder & Stoughton, p.164).

Agapē *means action*

In English we have only one word to express all kinds of love. The Greek language, in which the New Testament was written, is much richer. There are no fewer than four Greek words that bring out the various shades of the meaning of love. The commonest word used by the writers of the New Testament is the word *agapē*. The Holy Spirit inspired these writers to use this word, which became, as Professor William Barclay calls it, 'the very key word of New Testament ethics'. He defines *agapē* as 'unconquerable benevolence, invincible good will'.

> It is not simply a wave of emotion; it is a deliberate conviction of the mind issuing in a deliberate policy of the life; it is a deliberate achievement and conquest and victory of the will. It takes all of a man to achieve Christian love; it takes not only his heart; it takes his mind and his will as well (William Barclay, *New Testament Words*, SCM, p.22).

This is the love of God that has been poured into our hearts by the Holy Spirit if we are really children of God. It is a love that is to reach out beyond our circle of Christian friends, to our neighbour, to our enemies, to the whole world. The leaders of the early Christian church urged new believers to demonstrate the love of God in practical ways. If this sort of down-to-earth care was not evident in a person's life, then they challenged the reality of their experience of Christ.

> If anyone has material possessions and sees his brother in need but has no pity on him, how can the love of God be in him? Dear children, let us not love with words or

tongue but with actions and in truth (1 Jn 3:17, 18).

> What good is it, my brothers, if a man claims to have faith but has no deeds? Can such faith save him? Suppose a brother or sister is without clothes and daily food. If one of you says to him, 'Go, I wish you well; keep warm and well fed,' but does nothing about his physical needs, what good is it? (Jas 2:14–16).

Love is not just a warm, glowing feeling in a praise meeting. It is more than holding hands and singing *Bind Us Together* twenty times. It means more than meeting a fellow Christian in deep need, and 'assuring them of our prayers'. *Agape* means action! It means weeping with those who weep as well as rejoicing with those who rejoice. It means caring for them at your own expense. It means putting your interest aside for the sake of a brother in need.

You're a pilgrim not a resident

Men without Christ live as if this life were the only one that really counts, so they cram as much into their allotted time as they can possibly manage. People who know Jesus should know different. Men like Paul, Peter, James and John reminded the first Christian believers that they were a pilgrim people. This earth was just a stop-over point *en-route* to heaven. Because of this, things such as money and possessions should be held lightly and not grasped tightly. Pilgrims travel light, and are only weighed down by extra bits and pieces. Peter writes that the return of the Lord Jesus Christ will be sudden and unexpected. The earth will face his righteous judgement and, in the light of this, he poses an important question: 'What kind of people ought you to be? You ought to live holy and godly lives' (2 Pet 3:11).

As Christians, our lives in the here and now must always be lived in the light of the life to come. John warns:

> Do not love the world or anything in the world. If anyone loves the world, the love of the Father is not in him....The world and its desires pass away, but the man who does the will of God lives forever (1 Jn 2: 15, 17).

This does not mean that Christians should not work, get married, raise families and rent or buy property. We are positively told that to work and to provide for our needs, and the needs of those who depend on us, is a God-honouring duty. But the New Testament continually warns us against falling into the dangerous trap of being so in love with this world that we forget the reality of the next. God warns the godless rich that their oppression of the poor will soon be judged (Jas 5:1ff.) and he also warns his people to be awake and alert, ready for the coming day of Christ's appearance as Lord and King (1 Thess 5:6). Because of this truth, we are to hold our earthly possessions very lightly indeed so that when the time comes for us to let them go, we will hardly notice the loss.

The first Christians themselves

Jerusalem had never seen anything like it. Just weeks after the authorities had thought they had heard the last of Jesus of Nazareth the number of his followers had swelled to around 3,500 people. It is not as if they kept quiet about it either! Miracles, healings, open-air preaching and people suddenly beginning to praise God with a new-found joy and others speaking in languages they had never learned. The time-bomb of Pentecost caused a lot of damage. Luke, who wrote the book of Acts, gives a tantalizingly brief description of the sort of community life these Christians were living together in Jerusalem. In Acts 2:42–47, he provides an outline of their community life. He records that they displayed an extraordinarily generous spirit towards each other:

> All the believers were together and had everything in common. Selling their possessions and goods, they gave to anyone as he had need.

So read the two most embarrassing verses in the New Testament. God had invaded their hearts by his Spirit, and the reality of that invasion went right through to their pockets. This was no whipped-up religious 'trip' that Peter and the disciples had stage-managed. It was a response of gratitude to God for his salvation through Jesus and a new-found love for others who had joined his family. There was nothing compulsory or forced about this economic sharing; it came from hearts that were 'glad and sincere' because of all that Jesus had done for them. The thing that marked them out as changed people was the way that they *gave*. Just a few chapters later, Luke tells us, 'There were no needy persons among them' (Acts 4:34).

Such was the extent of their care for one another. This communal sharing does not mean that they rejected ownership of private property. As this verse goes on to explain, whenever a particular need arose, those who owned property or land would sell up and pass on the proceeds to meet that need. The tense of the Greek verb used indicates that this was an action that was repeated over a period of time, rather than a once-and-for-all sale. Luke tells us of Barnabas who voluntarily sold a field that he owned and gave the money to the apostles to be placed in the common fund. We are also told of Ananias and Sapphira, a husband and wife who continued together to hold back some money from a piece of property that they had sold. Their attempt to deceive the Holy Spirit resulted in their tragic deaths, an event that had a deep effect on the other disciples. It is interesting to note what Peter said when confronting the couple with their dishonesty. He makes it quite clear that the property belonged to Ananias and Sapphira; their decision to sell was a voluntary one. Even once it had been sold, the money still remained under their control. They could have decided to give part of the money, and openly admitted it. It is obvious that the sharing among the Jerusalem Christians was not compulsory but voluntary.

As in every growing church, problems arose among the Jerusalem believers. Luke records that a division occurred between two groups over the daily distribution of food to the widows in the fellowship (Acts 6:1ff.). The church leaders tackled the problem in a positive manner. They asked for seven spiritual men to be set apart for supervising this whole area of the church's life. Ronald Sider points out that every one of the men chosen had a Greek name, which indicates that the supervision of the scheme was handed over to the minority group that felt they had been discriminated against! There are some important lessons in this incident that we could do well to learn. Just think how many local churches could expand and grow if only leaders would be willing to delegate some of the tasks that God didn't even call leaders to do anyway. What an evangelistic impact on an area could be made if practical pastoral care was really practised by *others* in the fellowship and not merely left to 'the pastor'?

What happened in the Jerusalem church was special, but I do not think that God intended it to be unique. Church history bears witness to the fact that when the Holy Spirit moves in a mighty way he touches a man's heart as well as his head. How do you judge if a church is alive? By the prayer meeting? By the size of the Sunday congregations? I believe one telling indicator of a growing fellowship is the church accounts. If God is moving in people's lives then it will be demonstrated by their care for others and their practical commitment of money and possessions to the advancement of the kingdom. The example of what happened in the Jerusalem church in its early days is not a blueprint that we need slavishly to follow, but it stands as a powerful testimony of what can happen when God moves in people's lives. What happened in Jerusalem made people sit up and listen. The word of God was preached with authority because people could see a visible example of what it actually meant to be a citizen of God's kingdom. The evangelist did not just have to use words, he could point to living pictures of what it meant to be a child of God, and a member of his family.

I find that I come away from my New Testament feeling guilty and ashamed. When you consider the radical, self-giving discipleship that we read about within its pages and compare it with some of the discussions that go on in our church meetings and committees, you can be forgiven for wondering if it is all a dream. Peter faced the lame man at the gate of the temple and said, in effect, 'I don't have any silver and gold, but what I have got is spiritual authority.' He exercised that authority and the lame man walked. Today, the church in Britain looks at the morally lame, spiritually crippled and the materially poor and says 'We've got plenty of silver and gold (on deposit of course!), but what we haven't got is authority.' Because of this the crippled remain unhealed.

One of the greatest sins of the church of God in our nation for generations has been *meanness*. We have been mean in our dealings with our fellow Christians. We have been mean in our arrangement of the church accounts. We have claimed to worship the God who owns the cattle on a thousand hills, but we have acted as if at any moment he is due to go into voluntary liquidation. We have been mean in our care of God's servants, particularly those who have served on the mission field. We have been mean in our lack of practical concern for the plight of the world's poor. Most of all, we have been mean with God. Brokenness and repentance always lead to healing and forgiveness. I hope we are not too late.

4
Open Hearts and Open Hands

A. W. Tozer wrote about the supernatural growth of the early church in these terms:

> The (early) church was not an organisation merely, not a movement, but a walking incarnation of spiritual energy. The Church began in power, moved in power and moved just as long as she had power (A. W. Tozer, *Paths to Power*, Marshall, Morgan & Scott).

The first Christian disciples were scattered by persecution from Jerusalem, and as they went they carried with them the good news about Jesus. Within a few short years, living communities of the Christian 'way' had sprung up throughout the Roman Empire. Paul, the great apostolic church-planter, was kept busy, along with other leaders in teaching, preaching, and nurturing new converts as the gospel took hold of men's lives. The Jerusalem community was regarded as the 'mother' church by these fellowships as they traced their spiritual roots back to the city where it all began.

The believers in Jerusalem encountered severe problems in their early years. They were actively persecuted for their commitment to Jesus Christ. Added to this, there were severe economic problems caused by famine that ravaged Palestine. In a harsh financial climate many of the believers in Jerusalem found themselves without employment and facing deprivation. Other churches extended love to them in the form of financial aid. The church at Antioch received a prophetic message about a severe famine that they knew would hit hard at their brothers and sisters in Christ living in and around Jerusalem. They arranged a 'love-offering' and entrusted it to Barnabas and Saul (who was still serving his spiritual apprenticeship at that time) and they brought this practical expression of fellowship to the Jerusalem church.

As the years passed, the situation in Judea remained severe and Paul as an apostle arranged for a substantial collection to be taken among many of the churches across the Roman Empire. His object was to provide a large sum of money that would meet the needs of believers in Jerusalem who were suffering hardship. He wrote to the church at Corinth, on the subject of this great love-offering, and gave them practical directions as to how the money was to be raised. Rather than relying on a spontaneous whip-round, he urged them to set aside money systematically each Sunday as they met together for worship. Each person should determine how much to give in keeping with his income. By the time Paul arrived in Corinth, he expected a large amount would have been collected in this way, which in turn could be sent to Jerusalem along with the gifts from the other churches (1 Cor 16:1–4).

Several months passed between the writing of 1 Corinthians and 2 Corinthians, and there had been considerable friction between Paul and Corinthian believers. There had been deep problems in the church, and a barrier had come between them and Paul. He visited them in order to correct misbehaviour in the fellowship and to restore their relationship with the apostle. By the time 2 Corinthians came to be written the differences had been settled. In the stormy months that had passed, the collection for the church in Jerusalem had been forgotten, and in 2 Corinthians Paul urges the believers to remember their initial commitment to minister to the needs of their brothers and sisters in Christ.

It is interesting to consider this mammoth love-offering and to reflect on the feelings that lay behind it. On the surface there were striking differences between the Christians in Jerusalem and the other scattered churches. They were separated by distance; Corinth, for example, was 800 miles from Jerusalem. They were separated by racial divisions. The believers at Corinth were mainly Gentile converts while the Jerusalem church consisted largely of Jewish Christians. Most of them had never even met. In spite of these differences they were united together in the kingdom of God. God's persecuted people knew that they had to care for one another because in their hostile environment no one else would look after them. Ronald Sider draws attention to this remarkable vision of *interchurch* sharing (one group of Christians ministering to the needs of another group) as well as the early churches' capacity for *intrachurch* assistance (ministering to the needs of those within one fellowship).

The principle these believers had grasped was a basic but important one: if your heart is open to God then your hands will be open to your brother, wherever he may come from or whatever he may be like.

In 2 Corinthians 8 and 9 Paul gives practical instructions on the way in which this love-offering was to be arranged, and at the same time gives us an insight into how God wants us to look at the subject of giving. The Corinthian believers provide us with a useful case study of what it means to show practical responsibility for others in the body of Christ. We shall attempt to analyse and summarize Paul's teaching.

Paul draws the attention of the Corinthian believers to the churches in Macedonia (2 Cor 8:1–5). In modern geography, the Corinthians would have lived in southern Greece, while the Macedonians would have lived in the north. The 'Macedonian churches' were small communities of believers in places such as Thessalonica, Philippi and Beroea. They experienced harsh persecution because of their commitment to Christ and, added to this, most of them were extremely poor (v.2). Paul tells the Corinthian church of the 'overflowing joy' and 'rich generosity' that marked these Macedonian Christians. They urgently pleaded for the privilege of taking part in this tangible expression of love to the Jerusalem church. In a careful, pastoral way Paul is using the Macedonians as an example to the Corinthians as he challenges them to match this dedication to Christ. In my own visits to different parts of the world, and particularly behind the Iron Curtain, I have found without exception that it is always those who have the least who give the most. Our poverty-stricken and persecuted fellow believers around the world put us to shame by their open-handed generosity.

Having used the Macedonian churches as an example, Paul begins to deal with the subject of *real* giving.

1. The source of real giving

(a) God gives to us

Paul writes about the grace that God *gave* to the Macedonian believers (2 Cor 8:1). Every good work that we perform and every evidence of the fruit of the Spirit in our lives is because of God's grace at work in us. As Christians we are to see every act of love and kindness as coming from God's grace at work in our lives. The Macedonians were not acting out of a good-natured sense of generosity; it was God's grace at work in their lives that had produced this sacrificial giving. You can tell how far a person has gone with God by their giving. If this grace is working in their lives this is the type of fruit that will be produced.

(b) We give to God

The Macedonian believers 'gave themselves first to the Lord and then to us in keeping with God's will' (2 Cor 8:5). If we have experienced God's grace in our lives then our right response is to give ourselves fully to him. These believers had not responded to a high-pressure sales pitch about the needs in Jerusalem. They were not being emotionally blackmailed into making contributions. They were giving themselves, including the scant possessions that they owned, to the one who had given everything to them.

The source of real giving is when God's grace gets to work on our lives, releasing us from selfishness and fear. It is as we give ourselves first to the Lord in grateful response to his love that he opens our hearts and our hands to those around us in need.

2. The example of real giving

> For you know the grace of our Lord Jesus Christ, that though he was rich, yet for your sakes he became poor, so that you through his poverty might become rich (2 Cor 8:9).

Some of the deepest doctrinal truths in the New Testament are placed alongside plain teaching on practical living. In encouraging the Philippian Christians to not think just of their own interests, Paul uses the example of the humility of the Lord Jesus Christ, and in doing so provides us with one of the finest passages of theological truth that we have in our Bibles. The New Testament always links belief with behaviour and places doctrine and discipline side by side. The real example of giving is seen in God's gift of his Son for us. Jesus laid aside all the riches of his position in heaven, and willingly became poor in order that we may experience all the riches of being brought into God's kingdom. Jesus was 'the man for others'. His whole life was marked by sacrifice and characterized by the laying aside of self-interests.

The example is clear, and 'Whoever claims to live in him must walk as Jesus did' (1 Jn 2:6).

3. The standard of real giving

How much should I give? That is a question that, no doubt, the Corinthian believers were asking themselves. Paul does not give them a target, or suggest a fixed amount, nor does he indulge in 'keeping-up-with-the-spiritual-Joneses' tactics by revealing how much the Macedonians had given. The key to it all is our willingness. The gift is acceptable, irrespective of whether it is large or small, if it comes from a willing heart (8:12). For a man who only has £10, a £5 gift is a fortune, although it may look a pittance compared to the £50 gift given by a man whose savings total £5,000. With God it is the *attitude*, not the amount, that counts.

Paul goes on to explain that God wants to see *equality* among his people. Although the Corinthians are meeting the needs of the Jerusalem believers now, there may come a point when the situation is reversed, and then the giving will go the other way (8:13–15). That is a challenging concept to Western Christians and one that we need to face and grapple with. Paul quotes from Exodus 16, when God supplied manna for the children of Israel. Irrespective of whether a man gathered much or little of the manna, the shares were equal! If God was concerned about economic equality among his people in the Old and New Testaments, I wonder if his views on the subject can have changed much as he looks at the twentieth-century church?

4. The principle of real giving

Moving on a few verses and into Chapter 9, we discover a principle that relates to the Christian life as a whole, and not only to the question of giving: 'Whoever sows sparingly will also reap sparingly, and whoever sows generously will also reap generously' (2 Cor 9:6).

The measure with which you give will be the measure in which you receive. If you give yourself to the Lord, and to the service of others with an open heart, then you will experience the fullness of his blessing. On the other hand, if your Christianity is lived with a grudging attitude you will miss God's best for your life. Paul applies this principle while dealing with the subject of the love-offering. If you give with a generous heart, God will give back to you. Thousands of Christians have proved the truth of this principle in their lives: 'God is no man's debtor.' If you want a bumper harvest, make sure you are sowing plenty of seed.

For the past few years I have watched the lives of other Christians very carefully on this point. Basically, there are two types of believers I have found, the 'givers' and the 'getters'. The most fruitful and fulfilled Christians are always the 'givers'. They give of their time, their homes, their money, their possessions, their very selves. From what I have seen, they are the ones that are growing in God and experiencing his joy. These people are often totally free of the type of depression and spiritual introversion that betrays a self-centred believer. Of course they encounter pressures and problems as disciples, but their outgoing lives in meeting the needs of others preserve them from the sin of self-interest. The principle holds true: whatever you sow—you reap.

5. The motive of real giving

> Each man should give what he has decided in his heart to give, not reluctantly or under compulsion, for God loves a cheerful giver (2 Cor 9:7).

Paul touches next on the all-important issue of motives that lie behind our actions. The Corinthians should not be *careless* in their giving. The decision as to how much should be given must be given thought (and prayer) before the commitment is made. The decision must be a *personal* one, each person must make up their own mind and not be swayed by other opinions. A man should not be *reluctant* to give, there is no room for the 'I suppose I ought to' mentality. Similarly, there should be no *compulsion* about the offering. No one must be badgered into making a gift that comes from anything but a willing spirit.

Instead, we are to have in our hearts the motivation of cheerfulness that comes from a glad and carefree heart. The Greek word for 'cheerful' is *hilaros* which implies a ready and willing mind, a sense of joy that is willing to do anything. From it, of course, we derive the English word 'hilarious'. When you translate the verse 'God loves a hilarious giver', you get a better idea of its meaning. When was the last time you had people laugh in church when the offering came round? This is the same attitude of gladness and generosity that the Jerusalem believers had experienced (Acts

2:46). This was the attractive quality that drew spiritually hungry people to examine for themselves the message about Jesus. Hilarious giving is not just an instruction to first-century believers but is a characteristic of a son or daughter of God in any generation. Cheerfulness is the motive that should lie behind our giving because it delights the heart of God to see a ready, willing, joyful spirit in his children.

6. The blessing of real giving

In facing the Corinthian believers with the responsibility of giving, Paul is quick to point out the blessing that accompanies it (2 Cor 9:10–11). One of the sad things about Christians who fail in the area of stewardship of money is that they rob themselves of potential blessing. We have already seen the challenge that God gave to the nation of Israel through the prophet Malachi. He promised to open the floodgates of heaven if only they would get their priorities right (Mal 3:10). Although the Corinthians may find their love-offering a costly business, they could be assured that God would meet their own needs in full. Look at the words Paul uses to indicate God's capacity to bless: 'Supply...Increase...Enlarge...you will be made rich in every way'. Not only would God see to it that their needs would be met *materially*, he also promises that their lives would be enriched *spiritually*. This would enable them to continue to give to the Lord and enjoy seeing spiritual fruit growing in their own lives.

There was once a farmer who, as a committed Christian, gave fully and freely to the Lord. His recklessness in the matter of giving alarmed his friends who just could not understand how the man kept up this level of giving without going bankrupt. He was asked for the secret of his solvency. 'Well', he replied, 'as soon as I shovel out things to others, the Lord just shovels things back to me—and the point is, his shovel is bigger than mine!' That may sound trite, but it's true. How many of us miss out on the incredible blessing that belongs to those who take risks for God?

7. The outcome of real giving

In encouraging the Corinthian believers to approach the love-offering in a right way, Paul lists some of the clear benefits that will be the outcome of their obedience.

   (i) *The needs of God's people will be met* (9:12)
      When God wants to meet a need, he usually does so through the hands of his own people, allowing us the privilege of being his fellow workers.

  (ii) *Thanksgiving will be expressed to God* (9:12)

 (iii) *The Corinthians will have proved themselves to be obedient disciples* (9:13)

 (iv) *They will prompt prayer and promote fellowship* (9:13, 14)

In these verses Paul talks about their 'service', which literally means ministry. He also refers to their 'sharing' with the Jerusalem church, and the word used there is the word 'fellowship'. In being obedient to God in this practical way of meeting the needs of others, the Corinthians would be involved in ministry and experiencing fellowship in the fullest sense of the word.

In the last verse of the chapter (9:15) he reminds them not to lose sight of God's indescribable gift to us all—Jesus. Whenever we think of giving we must never forget how much we have been given.

In spite of their problems, the believers at Corinth had much to offer. Paul commends them for the way in which they excelled in faith, in their knowledge, in their gifts of ministry, in their earnestness to go on with God and their renewed love for Paul and his fellow leaders. But Paul urges them to go deeper still in their Christian experience that they may 'excel in this grace of giving' (8:7). James Denney commented on this verse:

> It is a real character that is suggested here by way of contrast, but not exactly a lovely one; the man who abounds in spiritual interests, who is fervent, prayerful, affectionate, able to speak in the Church, but unable to part with money (James Denney, *The Expositors' Bible*, Hodder & Stoughton, p.267).

If we want to grow up as mature sons and daughters of God, if we want to be a growing, Spirit-filled fellowship, then the 'grace of giving' is a target for which we need to aim. It is a *grace*, that is to say, it is Spirit-produced and not man-made, but if our lives are truly open to the influence of the Spirit of God, then this is a fruit he will want to produce.

Some practical conclusions

This case study on the church at Corinth provides important points that are relevant to God's people today.

First, giving is not treated here as an isolated subject, but as part of the whole business of growing and maturing in God. It flows from our walk with the Lord Jesus Christ, and if we are weak in this area of our Christian lives we are weak in the whole of our commitment. Paul does not tackle giving to the needs of others as an optional extra but as an essential ingredient in the life of a person totally given over to the lordship of Jesus. Perhaps we are willing to admit that giving is an underdeveloped area of our lives, but have we seen that this is an indication of our overall spiritual condition?

Another conclusion that we must draw from these chapters is that we have a responsibility to others in the body of Christ. That includes those within our own immediate fellowship, but it also includes members of the Christian family in other parts of the country, and the rest of the world. Are we as individuals, and as churches, willing to face up to this responsibility? Is it honouring to God that churches in our country carry forward a surplus in their accounts year after year while believers in other parts of the world remain in need? Ronald Sider comments:

> We live in a world dangerously divided between rich and poor. If a mere fraction of North American and European Christians would begin to apply biblical principles on economic sharing among the worldwide

people of God, the world would be utterly astounded. There is probably no other step that would have such a powerful evangelistic impact today (Ronald Sider, *Rich Christians in an Age of Hunger*).

Third, we should never be embarrassed about plain teaching and practical instruction on the subject of giving. Paul does not skirt around the issue but gives clear directions on the principles of Christian giving. To listen to some Christians approach the subject of money, you would think that their motto was 'Faith without hints is dead!' For years British ministers, missionaries and church leaders have talked privately about the pitifully low standards of giving in our country, but comparatively few have openly told the people who really matter—you and me!

One of the reasons that this book has been written is because of a conversation I shared with an American preacher at a Christian convention a few years ago. We were talking frankly about the alarming lack of support among British Christians for missionary work, as well as the generally low standard of giving in our churches. I asked where the fault lay, and was stopped dead in my tracks by his answer: 'It lies with you, and anyone else who gets into a pulpit in Britain. If you don't teach what the Bible says on the subject, they're not going to find out for themselves!' If we pride ourselves on new-found openness in our churches, then let us not be afraid to open up the way for clear teaching and honest discussion on this vital issue. We need patience with one another, particularly with those who are slow to catch up. We need love in our words, just as Paul firmly but gently led the Corinthians to face their responsibilities. We must be bold to face the issues that have been avoided for so long. It is not the 'big stick' approach that makes God's people begin to give, but a melting of the heart only the Holy Spirit can produce.

A fourth point for us to note is the importance that Paul attaches to our attitude of heart. We may find ourselves preoccupied with the amount we should give in a particular situation, but God puts the emphasis on our attitude. Can we honestly be described as 'hilarious givers'? Irrespective of how much is at our disposal to give away, do we approach giving with a sense of joyful recklessness? So often in our churches, the scrutinizing of the accounts is anything but a joyful experience. I am not advocating worldly carelessness in dealing with money that God has entrusted to us, but a little godly carelessness would not be a bad thing! The fact that our disposable income is high or low is not important; what matters to God is that the gift is accompanied by a right attitude. As one Christian graffiti artist has eloquently put it:

> It's not what you'd do with a million
> If riches should be your lot;
> But what are you doing today
> With the one pound fifty you've got?

Finally, it is worth noticing that Paul did not think it 'unspiritual' to challenge the Corinthians to thoughtful, systematic giving. On the contrary, he goes out of his way to suggest that each individual should make a clear decision as to what to give, and then add that to the love-offering on a weekly basis.

We have failed to be thoughtful and prayerful in our giving—partly because of Jesus' saying our left hand should not know what our right hand is doing when we make a gift, and partly because of a mixture of laziness and embarrassment. This is a mistake and, as Paul teaches the Corinthians, we must not run away from thinking things through carefully when it comes to giving to the Lord.

An open heart to God must always mean an open hand to others in need. For the early Christians this was not a concept to be argued over but one that needed to be acted upon. In order to have open hands to those around us we need first to release our grasp on the things we hold so tightly. Jim Elliot, a missionary to the Auca Indians of Ecuador, who was martyred in 1956 at the age of twenty-nine, was a man who knew much about the cost of following Jesus. He wrote these words in his diary:

> Father, let me be weak that I might loose my clutch on everything temporal. My life, my reputation, my possessions, Lord let me lose the tension of the grasping hand. Even, Father, I would lose the love of *fondling*. Often I have released a grasp only to retain what I prized by 'harmless' longing, the fondling touch. Rather, open my hand to receive the nail of Calvary, as Christ's was opened—that I, releasing all, might be released, unleashed from all that binds me now. He thought Heaven, 'yea,' equality with God, not a thing to be clutched at. So let me release my grasp (Elizabeth Elliot, *Shadow of the Almighty,* Harper & Bros, p.246).

Hands that are truly open must always be empty.

5

God's SAS

On May 5th 1980 a small group of hooded, armed men, clothed from head to foot in black, penetrated the besieged Iranian Embassy in the heart of London. Under cover of explosions and in a hail of gunfire, they shot dead five of the six terrorists who had seized the Embassy by force six days previously. The hooded rescuers secured the release of the nineteen hostages who had been held at gunpoint while the world looked on with bated breath.

Suddenly—not for the first time—the Special Air Service regiment of the British army was international news. But it was difficult to discover any details about the men themselves. This highly trained, resourceful team of tough soldiers carry out their duties anonymously. The very nature of their work demands that their exploits go mainly unpublished. Their regimental badge is a winged dagger striking downwards, bearing beneath it the stark motto:

'Who dares wins'

That would make a good motto for a Christian. The

Bible commends faith and makes it clear that without faith it is impossible to please God. If we examine the lives of great men and women of God in the Bible we discover that the very nature of their faith meant trusting God against the odds. In Hebrews 11 we find a comprehensive catalogue of some of the heroes and heroines in 'God's SAS'. We read of people who put their trust in the living God and overcame great obstacles with courage and daring. They forsook personal glory for his glory and put on one side the pursuit of personal pleasure in order to pursue God and please him.

In one sense, Hebrews 11 is an unfinished chapter. Throughout the centuries, right up to the present, heaven has been recording the exploits of faith undertaken by God's people. Today, in our materialistic society, God actively seeks out *extra*ordinary people who will be reckless in trusting him: 'For the eyes of the Lord range throughout the earth to strengthen those whose hearts are fully committed to him' (2 Chron 16:9).

Next to the Bible, the most important subject for any Christian to study is church history. In order to know God, we need to learn about him from the ways in which he has acted in the past. If we examine the lives of people who have been used by God we discover that, almost without exception, they have expressed their commitment in the area of possessions and giving. We are going to look briefly at a few examples. There are many lives that we could look at, but I have selected a few for no other reason than that these have been a personal blessing in my own Christian life and they have helped me in my understanding of the issue of giving. As with all Christian testimony, God wants us not only to be *challenged* by other people's lives but, by his grace, he wants us to be *changed* as well.

George Müller (1805–98)

George Müller was a Christian who became a national figure in his long and fruitful life. He was born in Prussia and first came to England as a missionary, working among Jewish people. God then led him to pastor a church in Devon, and later one in Bristol. It was during his time in Bristol that he founded his orphanage, for which he is best remembered. Earlier in his ministry he became convinced that God did not want him to receive a salary for his work, but simply to trust the Lord for the daily needs of his family. He had begun to learn many valuable lessons of faith and had proved the principle that 'those who honour me I will honour' (1 Sam 2:30). He carried the lessons he had learned into his work with deprived children. He established Sunday schools, published tracts and gospels, as well as opening homes for orphaned or unwanted children. He refused to advertise the financial needs of this valuable work, but operated on the principle that if God had called then he would provide.

Müller's great secret was not only his faith, but also his prayer life. He made his needs known to God. He built his life's work on the practice of faith in God expressed through prayer. The Bible played an important part in his life, and one verse particularly impressed him and moulded his outlook. The verse came from the teaching of Jesus:

> Give, and it will be given to you. A good measure, pressed down, shaken together and running over, will be poured into your lap. For with the measure you use, it will be measured to you (Lk 6:38).

George Müller reversed the usual Christian trend concerning giving. Instead of giving a proportion of his income to God, and then living on the remainder, he set a basic minimum amount for his personal needs—and gave the rest away. He once said, 'My aim was never how much I could obtain, but rather how much I could give!' The statistics of his ministry are challenging—particularly when you remember that this all took place 100 years ago. In the sixty-four years of his ministry with 'The Scriptural Knowledge Institution for Home and Abroad' (which was the title given to his work among children), the God of George Müller provided the penniless preacher with the following riches:

> He established five orphanages, giving a home to a total of 10,000 children at a cost of almost £1,000,000.
> He established seven day schools educating a total of 81,500 children.
> He established twelve home Sunday schools reaching a total of 33,000 children.
> The total cost of this part of his ministry was around £110,000.
> 2,000,000 Bibles and parts of Scripture were distributed at a cost of £42,000.
> 3,000,000 books and tracts were distributed, at a cost of £50,000.
> In addition approximately £26,000 was given away

to overseas missionary work.

In over sixty years of ministry God met the ministry needs of George Müller with approximately £1,500,000.

There were occasions when the last penny had been spent, and many children needed to be fed—but George Müller's testimony was that God always provided. One of his biographers has written:

> Such a life and such a work are the result of one habit more than all else, daily and frequent communion with God...prayer was the one resort, the prayer of faith.... He was an unwearied intercessor. No delay discouraged him. (A. T. Pierson, *George Müller of Bristol*, Nisbet & Co., p.302.)

He did not only pray for God to meet the considerable financial needs of his work, but he had a list of people who were regularly brought in prayer before the Lord. He prayed for people to be converted. Some he prayed for daily for one, two, three, six or even ten years. A year before his death he confided to a friend that there were two people for whom he had been praying daily for over sixty years. He added 'I have not a doubt that I shall meet them in heaven, for my heavenly Father would not lay upon my heart a burden of prayer for them for over three-score years, if he had not concerning them purposes of mercy.'

Some have criticized Müller for claiming to rely only on God, while allegedly dropping hints about the needs of his work to wealthy supporters. The following incident goes a long way towards refuting that sort of accusation.

Müller received a letter from a man who regularly supported the work of the Institution. The man asked directly 'Have you any present needs?' He went on to explain that he was not wanting Müller to move from his principle of non-advertising of needs, but he was asking a direct question as to the current financial position. Müller wrote a courteous reply:

> Whilst I thank you for your love, and whilst I agree with you that, in general, there is a difference between *asking for money* and *answering when asked,* nevertheless, in our case, I feel not at liberty to speak about the state of our funds, as the primary object of the work in my hands is to lead those who are weak in faith to see that there is reality in dealing with God alone.

A brave letter to write, particularly when you have only 27 pence in hand! The man who wrote the letter responded with a cheque for £100. The day the cheque arrived, there was not a penny left in the funds!

If you study his life, Müller appears in some ways to be an eccentric man. But when you consider his faith in God, you are left with the feeling that the eccentricity lies on our side of the fence. Many of God's great men and women appear strange to the world. Not many Ladies' Fellowships would want the prophet Amos to speak to them, particularly if he likened them all to 'Cows of Bashan'! John the Baptist would not be acceptable for Sunday school anniversaries. With his strange eating habits and the way he dressed he might frighten the children! As for the apostle Paul, once his prison record was made public he would never stand a chance of becoming a deacon or being elected to the parish church council. It is not only the world that finds some of God's special people 'strange', but sadly the church often follows suit. As someone once said, 'Often, when I call another Christian "a fanatic", what I really mean is that they love Jesus more than I do!'

Not everyone, at least in his day, dismissed Müller as an odd man. On the day of his funeral, the City of Bristol came to a standstill, as the people mourned the death of a great citizen. The Press wrote of him:

> Mr Müller occupied a unique position among the philanthropists of the nineteenth century. In an age of agnosticism and materialism, he put to a practical test theories about which many men were content to hold profitless controversy (*Bristol Evening News*).

> Thousands of children had been fed, clothed and educated out of funds which have poured in without any influential committee or organisations, without any appeal or advertisement of any sort. How was this wonder accomplished? Mr Müller has told the world that it was the result of 'Prayer'. The rationalism of the day will sneer at this declaration; but the facts remain, and remain to be explained. It would be unscientific to belittle historical occurrences when they are difficult to explain, and much juggling would be needed to make the Orphanages on Ashley Down vanish from view (*Liverpool Mercury*).

> Mr Müller's life and example, by their eloquent and touching beauty, cannot fail to impress even a sceptical and utilitarian age (*Daily Telegraph*).

> ...he was raised up for the purpose of sharing that the age of miracles is not past, and rebuking the sceptical tendencies of the time (*Bristol Times*).

We may be tempted to believe that George Müller was given a special measure of faith in order to carry out the particular job God had called him to undertake. That is not how Müller saw the situation:

> It is the selfsame faith which is found in *every* believer.... Oh! I beseech you, do not think me an extraordinary believer, having privileges above other of God's dear children, which they cannot have; nor look on my way of acting as something that would not do for other believers. Make but trial! Do but stand still in the hour of trial, and you will see the help of God, if you trust in him.

J. Hudson Taylor (1832 – 1905)

'A poor, unconnected nobody' is how some people saw the young man who was destined, under God, to become one of the greatest missionary pioneers in the history of the Christian church. Fellow Christians dismissed him as 'irresponsible', 'a hot-head', and 'unbalanced', but God owned and blessed Hudson Taylor's work and, through him, raised up a large missionary force to take the gospel to unreached areas of China.

Hudson Taylor was born in Yorkshire into a Christian home. His father had been deeply challenged about the spiritual need in China through reading several books. He knew he would never be able to go to China himself, owing to his family commitments, but he was led to pray that if God should give him a son, he might go to China with the good news of Jesus Christ. Being a wise father he did not share this desire with his son for many years. In fact, the young Hudson Taylor was so sickly as a child that no one ever expected him to undertake the arduous task of travelling to the other side of the world to serve God. He did not know of his father's prayer request until he returned home to England after his first seven years in China. Hudson Taylor underwent a deep conversion at the age of fifteen and some months later, when spending a free afternoon in prayer, surrendered his life and all his ambitions to the service of God. In his own words, he describes that solemn, sacred prayer time:

> I besought Him to give me some work to do for Him, as an outlet for love and gratitude; some self-denying service, no matter what it might be however trying or however trivial; something with which He would be pleased, and that I might do for Him who had done so much for me.... The presence of God became unutterably real and blessed; and though but a child under sixteen, I remember stretching myself on the ground, and lying there silent before Him with unspeakable awe and unspeakable joy.

Within a few months, the young Hudson Taylor was firmly gripped by the call of God to the vast and needy country of China. He began to read all he could lay his hands on about China, which, at that time, was a country with a handful of Christian missionaries. He was told of a local minister who had a book on China that Hudson Taylor wanted to read. He called on the minister to borrow the book and was asked why he wanted to read it. He told the older man that God had called him to be a missionary to the Chinese people. The minister was amazed and inquired as to how on earth he intended to get there. Hudson Taylor replied that just as Jesus had sent out his disciples without money or provisions for their journey, he was confident that God would meet all his needs. The minister placed his hand on the boy's shoulder and said, 'Ah, my boy, as you grow older you will get wiser than that. Such an idea would do very well in the days when Christ himself was on earth, but not now.' Many years later Hudson Taylor reflected on that conversation, and wrote:

> I have grown older since then, but not wiser. I am more than ever convinced that if we were to take the directions of our Master and the assurance He gave to His first disciples more fully as our guide, we should find them to be just as suited to our times as to those in which they were originally given.

The young Hudson Taylor did all that he could to make himself ready to serve God in a harsh and difficult country. Such preparation involved receiving some medical training as well as getting involved in evangelism and Sunday school work. In addition, he began to take regular exercise in order to build himself up physically and he tried to discipline himself not to live a comfortable life in order that he would be able to cope with the hardships of a foreign culture. He even changed his feather bed for a more basic model—a lesson from which we could perhaps all learn! Part of this process of preparation included a revolution in his life with regard to his giving. He earned very little as a medical assistant, but felt led by the Lord to give at least a tenth of his income to God. He even changed his digs, and moved to less comfortable accommodation, in order that he could faithfully give from his meagre income to the Lord's work. God led him to look at his wardrobe and small collection of books which resulted in him giving away unnecessary items. God dealt with him on the issue of giving and sowed seeds in the young Hudson Taylor's life that would bear much fruit in future years. He never lost the habit of regularly examining what he owned and how he used it and, in later years, he actively recommended that all true disciples of Jesus should do the same:

> If the whole resources of the Church of God were well utilised, how much more might be accomplished! How many poor might be fed and naked clothed, and to how many of those as yet unreached the Gospel might be carried!

God's preparation of Hudson Taylor for his future ministry took several years, until at the age of twenty-two years he set sail for China and arrived in Shanghai in 1854. At that time he worked with a group called the Chinese Evangelization Society. Through a series of events, Hudson Taylor severed his connection with this group and threw himself totally upon God for the financial support he needed. As he learned as a teenager, God never fails, and thus his work continued, supported by gifts and many miraculous provisions that the Lord gave in answer to prayer.

His methods were frowned upon by many, especially his insistence on dressing like the Chinese, and he was considered as a man who did not go by the book as far as being a 'good missionary' was concerned. Hudson Taylor preferred to go by *the* book and God honoured and blessed his sincere desire to make Jesus known. Ill health forced him to return to England, but he had not lost his burning desire to see China reached with the gospel. He founded the China Inland Mission (now known as Overseas Missionary Fellowship) and, incorporating the lessons of faith that the Lord had taught him, began to pray for a team of twenty-four missionaries to go into some of the unreached provinces of China. God gave him his vision and much more besides. Despite opposition (from fellow missionaries as well as powerful Chinese mandarins) and the heartfelt blow of the death of his wife, Hudson Taylor remained faithful to God's call and in thirty years he saw his team grow to almost 650 dedicated Christian workers. Many of the principles he learned and passed on to others have shaped and influenced the lives of missionary pioneers down to the present time. One of these key principles was absolute dependence on God alone to meet the financial needs of those who had been called to preach the gospel. He steadfastly refused to indulge in money-grabbing tactics and, although Hudson Taylor felt, on occasions, it was right to share openly the needs of the Mission, he believed that there needed to be a greater dependence on the Holy Spirit to prompt the Lord's people to give and less public appeals and pressure for financial support.

One incident from his life that illustrates this principle occurred a short time before he returned to China under the banner of the newly formed China Inland Mission. He had been invited to speak at a meeting on the needs of China. He stressed that he would only go if the advertising literature stated there would be no collection. At the end of the meeting the chairman rose to his feet and suggested that an offering should be taken, despite Hudson Taylor's request. People had been challenged and burdened to hear of the spiritual darkness in China and the chairman felt certain that the congregation would give a generous donation to the work. Hudson Taylor politely refused because he did not want people to give on the wave of an emotional response but said he would prefer people to go home and turn their burden into prayer, seeking God for what he wanted them to do to spread the gospel in China. His great concern was that these people were not given the false impression that the all-important thing was *money*, they needed to see the need of giving *themselves* to the work of God. Following the meeting, Hudson Taylor returned to the home of the chairman who, over a meal, made it clear that the missionary leader had made a mistake in refusing to allow a collection. The next morning the chairman arrived late for breakfast having slept very little through the night. He remarked to Hudson Taylor:

> I thought last night, Mr Taylor, that you were in the wrong about a collection; I am now convinced you were quite right. As I thought in the night of that stream of souls in China ever passing onward into the dark, I could only cry as you suggested, 'Lord what wilt Thou have *me* to do?' I think I have obtained the guidance I sought, and here it is.

He handed Hudson Taylor a cheque for £500 (a

considerable sum of money in 1866) adding that, if there had been a collection, he would have given a few pounds to it, but now this gift was the result of having spent most of the night in prayer for the spiritual needs of China.

Hudson Taylor was not being stubborn, but obedient. From his earliest days as a missionary God had taught him to depend completely on the heavenly Father who had called him to the work of preaching the gospel. The faith that filled the heart of the teenager when he told the minister that God would supply all his needs had been with him throughout the years of hardship and testing. There are many stories of God's remarkable provision for Hudson Taylor during those years and no doubt countless stories that are untold, until we get to heaven. The China Inland Mission was built on prayer and faith which should not lead us to praise Hudson Taylor and his colleagues, but to praise the living God who answered their prayers and honoured their faith. Over the entrance to the London office of the Mission there was engraved a text from the Bible that was special to Hudson Taylor: 'Have faith in God'. On either side of it, in Chinese characters, were written two other verses: 'Hitherto hath the Lord helped us' and 'The Lord will provide'.

His experience proved the truth of these words. He faced innumerable setbacks: ill health, the death of his wife, violent opposition, criticism and outright condemnation by fellow Christian workers, plus the inner fears and battles that face every spiritual leader. But he proved God. To reach the untouched areas of China required dedicated Christian workers. To support them, many thousands of pounds were needed. To penetrate the dark spiritual forces at work in China, much earnest intercession was required from Christians in Britain. The young man who learned how to give from a meagre wage packet to the work of God and laid *all* that he had at the feet of Jesus had come a long way in fifty years. But the essence of his faith was the same. It takes the same sort of faith to empty a wardrobe as it does to reach a nation.

C. T. Studd (1862 – 1931)

Charles Thomas Studd was a man whose life makes such remarkable reading that we could be forgiven for thinking that he was a story-book creation of the *Boys Own Paper* variety. He was born into a wealthy home and enjoyed the benefits of a privileged education at Eton followed by Trinity College, Cambridge. His father was a retired planter, who was converted through the ministry of the American Evangelist D. L. Moody. C. T. Studd became a Christian at the age of sixteen, but it was a few years later that the challenge of radical obedience to the claims of Jesus Christ met with full response from his heart.

He had risen to be a talented cricket player and played for England, touring Australia as a leading star of the side. On his own admission, he had grown cold in his heart towards God, and although he was surrounded by the glamour and appeal of being an internationally acclaimed sportsman, there remained an aching emptiness in his life. A battle for ownership was raging within him and he realized that he would never be truly satisfied until the lordship of Jesus was firmly established in his life. One of the great influences in his life at this time of crisis was a tract that he read, which had been written by an atheist. The unknown writer said that if Christianity was real, then those who professed to be followers of Christ would throw away all the comforts and pleasures of life in order to spread the good news. Every waking moment would be lived in the light of the life to come. If the claims of Christ were real, then one soul gained for heaven would be worth a lifetime of suffering. This cynical pamphlet made a deep impression on C. T. Studd. He later wrote:

> I at once saw that this was the truly consistent Christian life. When I looked back upon my own life I saw how inconsistent I had been. I therefore determined from that time forth my life should be consistent, and I set myself to know what was God's will for me.

This period of heart-searching led C. T. Studd to an experience of 'receiving the fullness of the Holy Ghost' as he described it later. This resulted not only in a powerful change in his own lifestyle, but also in God's blessing being experienced by thousands of people across the world who were touched by C. T. Studd's mighty ministry. He was led to volunteer for missionary service overseas, and as one of a group of students who became known as 'the Cambridge Seven' he stimulated and encouraged many other young people to commit their lives to the task of spreading the good news of Jesus throughout the world. He served in China as a missionary with the China Inland Mission and despite being sent home from the field owing to illness, he undertook a heavy programme of work in the USA where he urged and pleaded with Christian students to sell themselves out to the lordship of Christ. As a result, scores of young people were led by God to carry the gospel to those who had not yet heard of Christ. C. T. Studd then spent six years of fruitful ministry in South India where he pastored a growing church. Once again he was forced to return home owing to recurring illness. Undeterred by human weakness, he continued to preach and teach throughout Britain until, contrary to medical advice, he sailed in 1910 to Africa where he founded the 'Heart of Africa Mission', which later became known as the Worldwide Evangelization Crusade. He worked faithfully in Africa until his death at the age of sixty-nine years. He could have chosen a life of comfortable respectability at home, but his obedience to the lordship of Christ led to the ultimate blessing of thousands around the world.

Something that had a large part to play in the turning point of C. T. Studd's life had to do with possessions. He was due to inherit a substantial amount of money on his twenty-fifth birthday. This inheritance from his father's estate troubled him greatly as he weighed up the implications of a dedicated life. His study of the Bible had led him to the conclusion that his entire fortune must be given away. Although he was undoubtedly helped and influenced by men such as Hudson Taylor, with whom he freely discussed his thoughts, he realized that God was calling him to a simple step of childlike obedience to the black and white statements of Scripture. When his twenty-fifth birthday arrived, he was serving as a missionary in

China. He decided to give his fortune away. In order to complete the legal formalities he had to obtain the signature of a government official. The consul, who was no doubt alarmed at the implications of this move, refused at first to sign the necessary papers. He made C. T. Studd go away and think the matter over for a fortnight. Two weeks later he returned, resolute in his conviction that his entire inheritance had to be given away. The papers were signed and he gladly wrote cheques to the value of £25,000, sending the money to various societies and individuals for the cause of evangelism and the relief of the poor. He later wrote: 'God promised to give an hundredfold for everything we give to Him. An hundredfold is a wonderful percentage; it is 10,000 per cent!'

As the accountants set to work, investments were sold and gradually C. T. Studd's inheritance was given away for the work of the kingdom of God. He was left with £3,400. Just before his wedding he presented this money to his fiancée as a gift. She challenged him: 'Charlie, what did the Lord tell the young man to do—"Sell all"—well then, we will start clear with the Lord at our wedding.' They then sat down together and wrote a letter to General Booth of the Salvation Army. Part of the letter read as follows:

> We have felt the Spirit's drawing to this course after asking for a very long time 'To whom shall we give it?' Moreover, we have felt in this way we shall better reach the people, as being the Lord Jesus' way of coming to preach Salvation. Hallelujah! We can also thank God by His Grace that we have not done this by constraint, but cheerfully and of a ready mind and willing heart.

The young couple insisted that they wanted no one to know of this gift, and signed the letter:

> Your loving, we know, and getting humble, we trust, would-be soldiers of Jesus Christ. My Wife and Me.

The testimony of C. T. Studd and his wife, Priscilla, was that in forty-one years of married life and dedicated Christian service, the Lord never failed to honour their sacrifice or to provide for their needs and those of their children. They were obviously in love with one another. But their love for the Lord Jesus Christ was greater still. Before their wedding, C. T. Studd wrote to Scilla, as he called her:

> I love you for your love to Jesus, I love you for your zeal towards Him, I love you for your faith in Him, I love you for your love for souls, I love you for loving me, I love you for your own self, I love you for ever and ever. I love you because Jesus has used you to bless me and fire my soul. I love you because you will always be a red-hot poker making me run faster. Lord Jesus, how can I ever thank Thee enough for such a gift.

As the saying goes, 'The whole world loves a lover'. There is something wonderfully attractive about two young people deeply in love. Something more delightful by far to the heart of God is two young people in love with one another, but even more deeply in love with Jesus Christ.

It is said that if you want to discover the true measure of a man, then you should ask his friends what they think of him. Alfred Buxton worked alongside C. T. Studd in his ministry in Africa and was a close friend and co-worker. Following C. T. Studd's 'promotion' to heaven, he wrote:

C. T.'s life stands as some rugged Gibraltar—a sign to all succeeding generations that it is worthwhile to lose all this world can offer and stake everything on the world to come.

His life will be an eternal rebuke to easy-going Christianity. He demonstrated what it means to follow Christ without counting the cost and without looking back.

Sir John Laing (1879 – 1978)

One of this century's leading men in the support of Christian mission has been Sir John Laing.

He was a remarkable Christian. In his lifetime he succeeded in transforming a small business based in Carlisle into a large multinational corporation that is known throughout the British Isles. At the same time he gave away much of what he earned to Christian workers and institutions across the world. I have personal reasons for thanking God for the life of such a man. The theological college where I spent three of the most memorable years of my life in preparing for the Christian ministry owed much to the vision and generosity of Sir John Laing.

His life story makes challenging reading. As a young man of thirty his building business was in severe financial difficulty which heralded a spiritual crisis in his relationship with God. He made a commitment that he later 'described as the 'programme for my life'. He summarized it as follows: 'First the centre of my life was to be God—God as seen in Jesus Christ. Secondly, I was going to enjoy life, and help others to enjoy it.' He wrote his commitment down on paper and carefully carried it with him for the rest of his life as a constant reminder of his vow. In addition, he drew up a financial plan that was to govern his giving to God:

> Following a period of solemn prayer and dedication when in Barrow, I drew upon a sheet of Furness Abbey Hotel notepaper during September 1909 showing how I proposed to dispose of my income. That says:
>> If income £400 pa, give £50, live on £150, save £200
>> If income £2,000 pa, give £200, live on £500, save £1,300
>> If income £4,000 pa, give £1,500, live on £500, save £2,000.

He kept his solemn promise and, as the Lord blessed and prospered his business, he gave more and more back to the hands that provided for him. What is interesting to notice is that he covenanted with God that as his income increased, so his giving would increase while his own standard of living would remain at a certain level.

Fifty years after this turning point in his life, John returned to Furness Abbey with a friend and visited the spot where he had given himself in a new way to the Lord Jesus Christ. After a time spent alone in prayer, he walked back to his car and explained to his friend that this was the place where, at the height of his problems, he had sought God, and vowed that if he would show him the way through his troubles, he would make him a participating partner in his business. 'The Lord has kept his part of the contract,' he added, 'and I wanted to assure myself that I had kept mine.'

From the moment he allowed God to take the

central place in his life, John Laing began to see God at work in his life in a miraculous way. This is not a story of a man who lived in self-indulgent luxury, while handing out tax-deductible gifts to the odd charity. He saw that his personal prosperity had a purpose—that through his giving the kingdom of God could advance. Missionaries and Christian workers the world over were supported through his giving. People who need Jesus have first to hear about him. Without people to tell them, they cannot hear. If people are not sent, the message cannot be passed on. And those who are sent cannot live on fresh air! Because John Laing saw he was a child of God first and a businessman second, thousands heard the message of the good news of Jesus.

He was a modest man, who did not broadcast to the world the gifts that were made through his charitable trust to Christian work. He did not seek the limelight at Christian conventions. He sought personally to share the reality of Jesus Christ with those with whom he came in touch and was eager to be 'salt' and 'light' in his dealings in the business world. The day after his death in January 1978 *The Times* wrote:

> John Laing had a strong sense of responsibility for the welfare of his employees.

When his will was published, to the amazement of many, his net estate totalled £371. As his biographer wrote:

> The man who had handled millions had given them all away.

Professor Brian Griffiths commented:

> As a man who knew the reality of the spiritual world he
> never forgot that 'he looked for a city whose builder and
> maker is God'.

When Sir John Laing died, the Christian church
lost a front-line fighter through promotion. The
question remains, are there Christian men with this
sort of commitment who will fill the gap?

May Gage (1892 – 1978)

In this chapter we have briefly looked at a few house-
hold names of Western Christianity. Included in the
ranks of 'God's SAS' are thousands of unknown
heroes and heroines, who have demonstrated sacrificial commitment to the Lord Jesus Christ. Heaven
is a place where God's people will be rewarded and
openly recognized for their faithfulness. No doubt we
expect many of the great names to be richly rewarded.
I am stirred by the thought of the countless numbers
of anonymous saints whose reward will be far greater
than those whose lives are better known here on
earth. One such person will surely be May Gage.
You will probably never have heard of her before. I
would never have known anything of her life were it
not for the fact that while thumbing through a small
Christian magazine a few years ago I came across a
brief article under the headline 'From a Hut to a
Mansion'. Two full-time Christian workers who knew
May had written a brief and moving tribute to her
because of the challenge this quiet old lady had

brought to their own lives.

May Gage had lived for many years in an old wooden hut in Sussex, not because she was poor and neglected, but because she had made a deliberate choice back in the 1930s to give herself to a life of prayer and practical support for the Lord's work. She relinquished all the comforts of a normal home and moved into the flimsy wooden construction she humorously christened 'The Hut'. She took only the bare necessities in the way of furniture and settled down to a lifestyle that was austere and meagre to say the least.

She had a few small investments and she relied on the income from these to support herself. Her constant aim was to give as much as she could to the work of spreading the gospel. To ensure maximum possible support for the many individuals and societies she was interested in, she lived on a basic diet, with no room for luxuries. This remarkable lady was a keen gardener and grew flowers and vegetables to give away and sell to raise funds for various Christian projects. She saw her role in the kingdom of God as one of support for those in the front-line of the battle, but through her faithful prayers and sacrificial giving others were able to engage in spreading the gospel.

Her home measured 30 feet by 10 feet and consisted of a small kitchen, a living area and a small bedroom. There was no electricity, and a luxury she allowed herself later in life was a cold-water tap connected to the mains. Her means of heating was an old stove, fuelled by logs that she cut herself.

A Christian worker who knew May well wrote of her:

When you met with her you knew that you were in the presence of a woman who had discovered that Jesus was all in all. She had no need of anything else outside of the fellowship of the Saviour. Not a week passed that she did not prove the Lord in some way or another. She required a new pair of wellingtons...a friend arrived with a pair for her on the very next day...she needed a roof repaired and the need was met even before she asked. She proved that a person of prayer is a person of faith.

From time to time, she would examine her finances and decide what should be sold for the work of the kingdom of God. She would cash in her investments and give the proceeds away to a particular Christian work that the Lord had laid on her heart as she prayed. Those who knew her say she was a woman who had the character of Jesus. It is impossible to calculate this side of eternity what this lady gave to the support of Christian work, but thousands of pounds went from her open hands and all because she wanted others to discover the love of God in Jesus Christ.

At the age of eighty-six years she passed from a 'Hut to a Mansion', as the headline said. I felt stunned and very small when I read the brief account of her life. We immediately try to explain such actions away as 'eccentric' or hunt for some hidden quirk of character that betrays an unstable personality. The record stands. The details are not fully known on earth— but they are indelibly written somewhere in heaven.

I have no doubt that the disciples thought the woman with her expensive box of perfume was 'odd'. Jesus, in contrast, commended her lavish extravagance for he saw it as a costly act of worship. How many of the famous names will stand on the sidelines in heaven, when God's anonymous heroes receive *his* rewards and commendation?

We find ourselves in the same situation as the writer of the letter to the Hebrews who wrote: 'And what more shall I say? I do not have time to tell about...' (Heb 11:32).

We could talk about John Wesley, General Booth, Elizabeth Fry, Lord Shaftsbury—the list is endless. These are well-known lives in the history of the Western church, which is only a part of the worldwide body of Christ. No matter where we look, the central truth seems clear: men and women who have been used by God have been *givers*. At some point in their lives God has dealt with them on the issue of what they owned and how they used it. In God's school one of the first lessons that must be learned if we are going to be effective in serving him, is the lesson of *giving*. It is a basic building block that we must learn how to handle in the nursery section of Christian experience. God may entrust you with much by way of possessions, or he may give you little. The amount is unimportant. What matters is how we use what he has given.

What are you doing with the possessions God has entrusted to you? How does the lordship of Jesus Christ affect your use of money? Are you really concerned to see 'Thy kingdom come, thy will be done, on earth as it is in heaven'? If so, how does your giving match up with your praying?

There is room in the ranks for more heroes and heroines of faith. Men and women are needed in our generation to be willing to radically re-examine their lifestyles and values in order to do great things for God.

For further reading

George Müller

Roger Steer, *George Müller: Delighted in God* (Hodder & Stoughton)

A. T. Pierson, George Müller of Bristol (Pickering & Inglis)

J. Hudson Taylor

J. C. Pollock, *Hudson Taylor and Maria* (Kingsway Publications)

A. J. Bromhall, *Hudson Taylor and China's Open Century* (Hodder & Stoughton/Overseas Missionary Fellowship)

C. T. Studd

Norman Grubb, *C. T. Studd: Cricketer and Pioneer* (Lutterworth Press)

Sir John Laing

Roy Coad, *Laing* (Hodder & Stoughton)

6

Hilarious Giving

There is a cash crisis in the British church. The fault lies as much with the pulpit as it does with the pew, but now is not the time for apportioning blame. God is calling us to acknowledge our failure, confess it to him and get on and act to put the situation right. The crisis has affected every area of our life and witness as the body of Christ. Here are some of the most seriously affected areas.

The ministry

Most ministers, whatever their denomination, are overworked and underpaid. That is part of the price to pay in any vocation that is, in the true sense, 'a calling'. No one should enter the ministry with a view to financial security. The fact remains that most of the major denominations that fix a basic minimum stipend for their clergy admit that it is below the level they would like to set if giving from the churches was more realistic. Of course, we can argue that ministers often receive fringe benefits such as a church house, help with running a vehicle, telephone costs, etc.

Even so, we have to face the fact that there are ministers and their families up and down the country who rely on the state to supplement their income, because they are adjudged to be at such a low level of financial support. Should we expect the welfare state to be doing the job of the local church? The New Testament challenges us with these sort of words:

> Don't you know that those who work in the temple get their food from the temple, and those who serve at the altar share in what is offered on the altar? In the same way, the Lord has commanded that those who preach the gospel should receive their living from the gospel (1 Cor 9:13,14).

> The elders who direct the affairs of the church well are worthy of double honour, especially those whose work is preaching and teaching (1 Tim 5:17). [The word 'honour' is connected with the idea of financial remuneration.]

Recently I met a colleague of mine who is a minister. He told me that his church had just met to consider his salary and whether it should be increased. The result was that the church decided to *cut* his annual income by £300 per annum! The reason was that they had seen how their particular denomination intended to raise the level of ministers' support over the next few years, and they decided they could not afford it. That story is, sadly, typical of the sort of attitudes that exist in some of our local churches. Whatever happened to faith? There are ministers who *are* well cared for by their churches, but for every one of those there are twenty who are struggling by at an appallingly low level of support.

There are a number of questions you may be asking at this point: 'What if the congregation is poor or has many non-wage-earners in membership?' 'Surely the call to the ministry is a call to a life of self-sacrifice?' 'If ministers don't complain—the problem can't be serious?' Such questions are legitimate, but they do tend to lead us away from the heart of the matter. Every committed member of a truly Christian church should ask themselves the question: 'Are we supporting God's servant to the best of our ability, and in a way that is pleasing to the Lord?'

Missions—at home and abroad

I will never forget an encounter several years ago with two American missionaries. I was visiting a part of the world that could be described as 'the front-line' so far as the mission field is concerned. They were perplexed because one of their colleagues, a British missionary, had returned home from the field with his family. He was a skilled linguist and, in the area of personal evangelism, had made some real breakthroughs in a strongly anti-Christian culture. His fellow workers saw that this brother had a rare gift for communicating Christ in the language of the people. The reason that he and his family had to return home was due to the low level of support they were receiving from Britain. He, his wife and children had been living on a starvation diet at times and heavily relied on fellow missionaries for support, as well as borrowing money from national Christians. The pressure of this situation produced deep problems for the family, both material and spiritual, and after many months of heart-searching, the decision was made for them to withdraw. I was one of the only British Christians these American missionaries had met since the departure of their friends. I stood that day as a representative of the British church and faced a barrage of questions. There was no sense of spite in what they said, just expression of amazement that such a situation could continue for so long unchecked. 'What's wrong with British Christians?' they asked me. I had plenty of excuses, but no real answers.

In the situation that I have just outlined there are other factors to be borne in mind. The missionary society that sought to provide a covering for this particular family, to say nothing of the responsibility of the local church who sent them out in the Lord's name—these areas were undoubtedly a little at fault in this sad story. But the fact remains that our support for overseas missions is well below what it should be. Those who examine the statistical evidence inform us that, beyond doubt, overseas missions are the Cinderella of Christian witness.

But when we look at support for home missions, the situation still gives cause for concern. Many of us are prompted to give to those situations that touch our hearts. If I were to arrange a meeting in my own home town on the subject of 'Persecuted Christians behind the Iron Curtain', I would be guaranteed a packed hall and a large offering. But if I put on an evening meeting concerned with 'How to Support a Full-time Christian Schools Worker', the turnout would be minimal. Somehow we feel that the mission field starts the other side of the English Channel. We fail to understand the spiritual darkness on our own shores. There are various groups engaged in unspectacular ministries in schools, colleges, prisons, villages and all sorts of places throughout Britain. Leaders of such groups face the continual frustration that they cannot expand and develop their ministry in the way that they believe the Lord wants them to, owing to lack of regular, committed financial support.

Standards of living and standards of giving

There have been great changes in British society in the past twenty or so years—not least in our level of income and how we spend it. The table overleaf makes interesting reading. No doubt the first fact that most of us will pick up is that our income tax bill has shot up in twenty years! Set alongside these figures is the staggering fact that our average giving to Protestant missionary societies is running at *15p* per church member per week! In twenty years our income has risen, and so has our expenditure, but what about our *giving*?

In a recent article a leading Christian magazine reported that many home and overseas missions are in a state of severe financial crisis. Their overheads have increased. They are having to support missionaries who are living in countries with high rates of inflation, but sadly most of us as British Christians think in terms of pennies rather than pounds when it comes to giving.

Nowadays most of us expect (rightly or wrongly) that if we are in the privileged position of earning a wage, then it should be reviewed on an annual basis.

What we earn and how we spend it

Commodity	Average income and expenditure in 1960 £	(%)	Average income and expenditure in 1980 £	(%)
Average WEEKLY INCOME	20·39	(100)	134·08	(100)
Tax and saving	3·23	(15·8)	31·53	(23·5)
Average WEEKLY EXPENDITURE				
Housing	1·54	(7·6)	15·17	(11·3)
Fuel, light and power	1·62	(7·9)	5·7	(4·3)
Food	5·04	(24·7)	23·52	(17·5)
Alcoholic drink	0·52	(2·6)	4·96	(3·7)
Tobacco	0·97	(4·8)	3·09	(2·3)
Clothing and footwear	1·70	(8·3)	8·41	(6·3)
Durable household goods	1·05	(5·1)	7·38	(5·5)
Other goods	1·17	(5·7)	8·05	(6·0)
Transport and vehicles	2·01	(9·9)	14·66	(10·9)
Services	1·47	(7·2)	10·86	(8·1)
Miscellaneous	0·07	(0·3)	0·75	(0·6)

Needs change; our expenditure rises with inflation and also our pursuit for a better standard of living. We need to ask, as God's people, if it is right for us to get caught up in such a rat race. Another important question for us to face concerns the level of our giving. Does our giving increase in keeping with the money that we earn? For those who are dedicated 'tithers' the answer is an easy one—the tenth increases in pace with the whole. But if, for whatever reason, you do not tithe, do you review regularly and prayerfully what you give and where you give to?

A useful and challenging exercise for any of us who claim to live under the lordship of Jesus would be to break down our expenditure into the sort of detail indicated in the table, adding to the list a category entitled 'Giving'. Compare how much you spend on yourself with how much you give to the Lord. Mr Average Non-Christian seems to spend more on alcohol and tobacco than many of us give to the cause of Christ! Voltaire, the atheist philosopher, once remarked that Protestantism is merely a less expensive substitute for Catholicism. If you want to know what really matters in a man's life, take a look at what he spends his money on.

When we examine the proliferation of cults and new religions that have emerged in the past century, one of the distinguishing features of these groups is their willingness to give to their particular cause in a sacrificial way. What a rebuke to our easy-going *churchianity*. The cults are growing owing to their aggressive zeal in winning new converts and the wholehearted dedication of their members to give until it hurts. Look at some of the more extreme political parties that are around today. We may be a million miles from their views, but few of us can fail to feel ashamed at the commitment they display in tramping through rain-drenched streets campaigning for their candidates. If you believe in the revolution —you give. The words of C. T. Studd challenge us again: 'If Jesus Christ be God and died for me, then no sacrifice can be too great for me to make for Him.'

Personal giving

Let us turn to some of the practical questions involved in giving to the Lord. I have already suggested that we need to make a careful examination of our income and expenditure, particularly looking at how much we give to the Lord. If you realize that you have not been giving as you should, then the place to begin to put things right is by acknowledging your sin (for that is what it is) before God. Seek his forgiveness and trust him to teach you the right use of the gifts he has entrusted to your care. Repentance means putting right things that are wrong. This is the next step, and we are going to look at some of the practicalities involved.

How much should I give?

We have already seen how the practice of tithing (giving one-tenth) is recorded in the Old Testament. Long before the law was given, Abraham tithed. The principle of tithing was incorporated into the law as given by God to Moses. As we have mentioned previously, the Israelite gave more than the tithe to the Lord; that was only the beginning of his giving. A more realistic assessment of the tithes and offerings he would be expected to give amounts to a staggering 23½% of his total income.

'To tithe or not to tithe' has been a debate amongst Christians for many years. Some have objected to tithing as a legalistic hangover from the Old Testament, while others have insisted that, like the law in regards to matters such as murder and theft, the principle of tithing abides for all who are true disciples of Christ. To engage in fierce debate on such a matter is akin to a group of passengers aboard a sinking liner, arguing about the finer details of coastal navigation. Each of us must seek God in prayer and through his word on the matter.

My personal conviction is that tithing for a Christian is firstly a *guideline*. Secondly, I believe that the tithe for the Christian is a *basic minimum* so far as giving is concerned. Many of the early church leaders came from a Judaistic background and would have been conscientious in the matter of their tithes and offerings. As we have already noted, one of the hallmarks of the Christian community in Jerusalem was their spontaneous, overwhelming generosity in giving. Luke tells us that this made even the Jewish population, who were givers, sit up and take notice. In his helpful book *Tithing*, Dr. R. T. Kendall writes:

> God does not enforce tithing today. But to the person who is under Christ's law there will be given—sooner or later—the light of tithing, God's way. When we are given the light of tithing, we show at that moment whether or not we submit to the yoke of Jesus Christ. (R. T. Kendall, *Tithing*, Hodder & Stoughton, p.62).

In all matters in our Christian lives, we must be obedient to the light that God has given us. While preaching at a church in Wales several years ago, a young man spoke to me after the evening service. He was training in the Royal Air Force, and had been converted to Christ for just a few weeks. He was eager to ask questions about growing in God. One issue that had disturbed him as he read his newly acquired Bible was that the New Testament Christians had obviously been givers. He knew that God was calling him to give too, as a demonstration of his commitment. The problem that he was wrestling with was 'How much?' He told me, 'I have been praying about this for several days, and I feel the Holy Spirit is telling me 10% of my wage must be set apart for the Lord—does that sound all right to you?' That young man in two weeks had travelled further than some Christians do in twenty years. Without any outside intervention, the Holy Spirit had given him the 'light of tithing'. I urged and encouraged him to *begin* there and test out the biblical injunction to 'prove God'. Sadly, some of us who may well be tithers feel tempted to congratulate ourselves and believe that we have nothing more to learn on the subject of giving. We do well to remember the words of the Lord Jesus. 'So you also, when you have done everything you were told to do, should say, "We are unworthy servants; we have only done our duty"' (Lk 17:10)

The answer to the question 'How much?' will come to us when we are on our knees. The Lord may convince you that the tithe is right for you in your current situation. Or he may lead you like John Wesley, Sir John Laing and others to the conclusion that you need to give far more by reducing your own living expenses. Those of us on low incomes must not feel inferior because our gifts appear so small. The story of Jesus and the widow at the temple treasury reminds us that God looks to the commitment in our hearts that accompanies our gifts, be they large or small.

A question that often arises concerns income tax and other deductions from a wage-earner's pay packet. Should I calculate my tithe (or whatever proportion God leads me to give) from the 'gross' or the 'net'? Once again, this is a matter that we must commit to prayer for the Holy Spirit's guidance. From a personal viewpoint, I believe we must consider the gross amount of our income as the total that God has entrusted to us. When we consider how those deductions are used we realize that even though they represent money taken out of our pockets, they serve to provide for the benefits we receive within the welfare state. Jesus reminded us to give to Caesar the things that are Caesar's (i.e. taxes) and to God the things that are God's. It is morally right for a Christian to pay income tax and we have a duty to uphold the right of the state to govern. As we ultimately derive benefit from money given over to the state, it seems only right that we consider the *whole* of our income as belonging to the Lord.

We need the help and direction of the Holy Spirit to lead us to know how much we should give. In the light of his guidance, through careful study of Scripture, we must then give ourselves to carrying out our responsibilities faithfully.

One further word needs to be added. *Reviewing* our

giving is an important matter. There are times when it is right to give a special thank-offering to the Lord. This Old Testament practice is a valid pointer for twentieth-century believers. If God prospers you in a particular way, through receiving perhaps a bonus or extra payment of some description, it can be a wonderful opportunity to worship the Lord with a gift over and above our normal offering. Let us not fall into the trap of becoming 'rusty' in our giving. A person who is open to the lordship of Christ will always be ready to increase their level of giving as circumstances change.

To whom should I give?

It is worth repeating Paul's comment to the Corinthian church about the generosity of the believers in Macedonia: 'They gave themselves first to the Lord' (2 Cor 8:5). Our giving, wherever it may be directed, must be *to the Lord*. We must recognize that we are involved in an act of worship. Paul linked the setting aside of a regular sum of money with 'the first day of every week' (1 Cor 16:2) which was the day that the Corinthians met together to worship the Lord. How much richer and meaningful our praise and prayer becomes when accompanied by the gifts of God's people.

All of us, the disciples of the Lord Jesus Christ, have a duty to give *to the local church*. The New Testament gives no brief to spiritual nomads who prefer to hang loose rather than be identified and committed to a localized body of Christian disciples. It follows that we have an obligation to give where we worship. We have a duty to support those who lead and teach us, as well as to contribute to the upkeep and running costs of the church. Most local churches are involved in the support of missionaries and outside Christian agencies, and it follows that our gifts should be channelled, via the fellowship, to meet such needs. We shall consider later how we need to be informed and involved as to how local church funds are used. There is a strong school of thought today that takes the view that the 'storehouse' (see Mal 3:10) is the local church, and that the whole of a Christian's apportioned gift should be directed there. It is then the duty of the local church to support missionary societies and other groups. R. T. Kendall writes:

> The Church has lost its credibility in the world. To give the actual tithe, God's tithe, to any organisation other than the (local) Church is to perpetuate the loss of credibility which the Church has suffered. Were every Christian to tithe directly to the Church, it is my view that every Christian organisation which is owned by God would have more than ever (R. T. Kendall, *Tithing*, pp.80–81).

I believe there is much to commend the view that our tithe should be directed to the local fellowship, and that our offerings (i.e. giving over and above the tenth) should be given direct to outside individuals and organizations.

When it comes to prayer and financial support, we have a responsibility to be involved in the area of *missions abroad and at home*. It may well be that we have personal contact with missionaries or full-time Christian workers, serving God in Britain or overseas. It is always easier to pray for people we know rather than just an anonymous organization. Most missionary societies run a sponsorship scheme that enables Christians to give a regular amount for the support of a particular individual. For too long, active, practical interest in missions has been left to the precious few in local churches. Every Christian should be involved in mission. We are desperately ignorant about the needs and opportunities in the world today. A lesson from my own experience has been: if I give, I pray. One way to stimulate our prayer life in the area of world mission is to become committed financially to the support of those involved in the task of sharing the gospel.

Books and messages in recent years have challenged us to remember the *needs of the poor*. Men like Ron Sider and others have done much to stir and stimulate our thinking in this area. In our affluent, Western society, we often hear complaints about the erosion of our standards of living. Christians should play no part in the voicing of such protests. We have so much, while many have so little. John Wesley once wrote to his tax inspector telling him that he owned two silver spoons—one in London and one in Bristol. He added that he would never own more 'while men around me still need bread'. I was in the middle of writing this book when I made my first visit to the vast sub-continent of India. Two days before I left home I had led my church in our harvest festival celebrations. I watched my own children proudly walk to the front to add their gifts to our bulging display of produce, until the front of the church looked like a supermarket. Within forty-eight hours I sat in a taxi in the slums of Bombay watching half-naked children, soaked and shivering in a violent storm, putting their hands through the open windows of cars begging for a few rupees. One boy who approached me was the same age as my eldest son. I felt something that day of the pain of God's heart. If the plight of the poor does not move your heart, then you understand little of the heart of God. In our regular giving we must remember the needs of the poor, just as the early church set that as a priority target in their mission to the world.

We have already seen how the word *fellowship* involves giving. For a church to be truly a family, there needs to be mutual caring and sharing. In our giving we must not neglect *those in need around us*. Every local church has people in need, whether in the fellowship or within the surrounding community. These people provide us with daily opportunities to demonstrate the love of Jesus. Many churches have a 'fellowship needs fund' from which gifts may be made, on behalf of the church, to those in genuine need. But this is just the start. Look around your own church with open eyes and you will find people that you can bless through your giving. We once belonged to a fellowship where a young married couple with a small family were experiencing severe financial difficulties. Some of the leaders met with the husband to pray and go through his financial situation. Having made sure that the family were handling their money correctly (some of us do need help on such basic matters), the leaders concluded that, owing to circumstances out of their control, the family would not be able to make ends meet for several months. The problem was shared and wage-earners in the fellowship volunteered to help the family on a regular basis. To prevent unnecessary embarrassment, one of the leaders took on the responsibility of collecting the contributions each month and passing them on. The family was blessed, and they grew in God. The fellowship was blessed and the Lord used the situation to speak to non-Christian members of the wider family. Above all, I believe the Lord was blessed, because he saw his children taking commitment to one another very seriously indeed.

In the church where I am now part of the pastoral team, my senior colleague laid down an important principle some years ago. 'If you are in genuine need,' he told the church, 'when the offering plate comes around, feel free to take something out rather than feeling forced to put something in.' He was not joking. Caring must always mean sharing.

How should I give?

There are always dangers in being dogmatic. But in order to answer some of the practical questions I have faced myself, and sought to help others with in counselling, I want to suggest some guidelines for giving.

(i) *Pray before you give.* It is important to seek the face of God concerning the direction of our gifts. If we are truly giving to him, then it must follow that the Lord knows where that money is needed most. We can be guilty of merely giving on the basis of an emotional response to a pressing need. There is something spiritually rewarding in giving to someone, or to a particular need, because the Lord has burdened you with a strong sense that this is where your gift is to go. In kingdom economics, we are often wonderfully blessed to discover that our gift arrived at exactly the right moment to meet a particular need, despite the fact that we had no prior knowledge of that need. Such is the privilege of being fellow workers with God.

(ii) *Develop a system of giving.* Most of us tend to be undisciplined as human beings and we need structure and order to bring out the best in us. If we are not careful, such a lack of discipline can lead us to neglect God in the matter of giving. Most of the counselling situations that I have been involved with focus on this point. However 'unspiritual' it may seem to you, most of us need to develop a system of giving. Systems vary, some have found it useful to take out of their weekly/monthly wages the amount set aside for the Lord and to put it in a special place such as an envelope, or cash box. Others open a separate account to which they regularly transfer their portion of income dedicated to the Lord. This account is seen as belonging to the Lord, that is to say, utterly devoted to him and for use only as he directs, and from it regular gifts are made. A number of Christians have found it useful to keep a written record of their gifts—not on the basis of being proud of their good works, but in order to ensure that they are able to keep track of the level and direction of their giving. Find a method that suits you. Obviously factors such as how often you are paid will influence you, but discipline yourself to stick to your system. Whatever you decide, make sure that the 'Lord's portion' is what comes out of your income *first*. Refuse to be sidetracked into leaving God's share until everything else is paid.

Seek his kingdom first and he will honour you for it.

(iii) *Determine your regular commitments*. Discover from God where your regular commitments lie, and how much of your giving should be allocated in such directions. As we have already noted, top of this list should be the local church. In addition, you may find that the Lord leads you to have a regular commitment to an individual or missionary society. Regular, committed giving is much needed by such groups who have to face continual demands on their resources.

(iv) *Use a Deed of Covenant where possible*. In this connection, local churches and Christian organizations that are registered charities are able to claim from the Inland Revenue tax at the standard rate on gifts which are made under a Deed of Covenant.

I have met Christians who believe that such a scheme is morally wrong because it implies avoiding income tax, and others have suggested that it denies the principle that our giving should be done in secret. Neither view holds up under fire. The trouble is that we are afraid of committing ourselves to regular giving, and we feel that if nothing is in writing, we can always withdraw our support. We live in the privileged situation that the law allows charities to make extra income, if their supporters are willing to sign a Deed of Covenant.

To give a practical example: if the tax rate was 30%, and you paid tax on your salary at that rate, you can choose to pay to your church or other Christian charity £70 per year. If you decide to make that gift by Deed of Covenant, the church or charity can immediately claim back £30 from the Inland Revenue. This makes your original gift of £70 worth £100!

Most churches and missionary societies would prefer all gifts to be made in this way, as it would mean a significant increase in their regular income. For many it would mean the difference between sinking or swimming.

To enter into a Deed of Covenant, you need to complete and sign a simple form in the presence of a witness (two witnesses are required in Scotland). These forms can usually be obtained from a church or missionary society on request. A Covenant must be for a period of not less than four years but, if you choose, it can be for a longer period of time. Should you die then the Deed is automatically cancelled.

A group called the Charities Aid Foundation* runs a scheme where you are able to enter into a Covenant with them, and, at your request, they will send the gross value of your gift to the individual charities of your choice.

(v) *Keep a portion of your gift for 'special use'*. While regular commitments in giving are important, some Christians have found it useful to keep a portion of their gift for 'special use'. Regularly we are faced with emergencies that occur, both in an international and local sense. In such situations it is a privilege to be able to minister to those emergency needs. You may find it useful to put such sums into a special place or account. Also, it is a helpful spiritual exercise to be praying and looking for areas of financial need. It teaches us to think of the interests of others and develop a sensitivity to God's prompting voice.

---

*Charities Aid Foundation, 48 Penbury Road, Tonbridge, Kent TN9 2JD. Tel: Tonbridge 356323.

(vi) *Pray as you give*. If we simply give the Lord's money to our church or elsewhere, and do not pray, then we have missed a large part of the point. We give, as to the Lord, to see his kingdom built. That will not simply be achieved by finance and manpower. Supremely, our task is one of prayer. Pray for people who are on the receiving end of your gifts. Learn to pray strong prayers on their behalf. Cry to the Lord for blessing and an outpouring of the Holy Spirit on their ministry. Never lose sight of their spiritual needs while you are ministering to their practical needs. There have been times in our own ministry when my wife and I have received a letter with a personal gift enclosed. Sometimes the donor (often anonymously) has enclosed a letter of encouragement, saying that they have been praying for us and perhaps they have shared a scripture that God has laid on their hearts. If ever you have been on the receiving end of a letter like that you will know the encouragement is more appreciated than the gift!

(vii) *Review your giving regularly*. Refuse to stand still in your service of giving to the Lord. Regularly you need to look through and pray about how much you give and where it is directed. Those who keep a written record of their gifts find that their system is most helpful in this respect. Obviously, we need to avoid the danger of becoming erratic by constant changes, particularly where we are supporting people (such as missionaries) who are dependent on our regular gifts.

(viii) *Give cheerfully*. Remember that 'God loves a cheerful giver', so give gladly and not grudgingly. Our giving to the Lord should be seen as a delight and not a drudge. So often we read in Scripture of how God looks into our hearts to discover our attitudes. As you give, thank God for the privilege of bread to eat, and a bed to sleep in. Root out of your heart any sense of resentment about giving and do it with a thankful attitude. Do that, and you will grow visibly in your Christian life.

'But my income is so small—surely God can't expect me to give like this?' someone might ask. Surprising as it may seem, experience proves that those who have the least are usually those who give the most! It may well be that you have only a small pension, a limited student grant or unemployment pay on which to survive. God understands about economic difficulties, but he invites us to prove his ability to meet all our needs. Following a series of sermons on the subject of giving in my church, I received a letter from one of our young married couples. They told me that they had previously taken the view that sacrificial giving to the Lord was something that applied later in life—once the pressures of having a young family had passed. God had now challenged them on the issue of trusting him. They decided together to step out in faith and put God's kingdom first on their agenda. Some months later, they confided in me their amazement at how the Lord had made less money go further than ever before. In addition, they were experiencing a sense of joy at being released from possessing their possessions. They told me, 'Put it this way, we've learned that we can't afford *not* to give!'

If you wait until you are financially secure before you give, then you are not really *giving*. As King

David (the man after God's own heart) put it: 'I will not sacrifice to the Lord my God burnt offerings that cost me nothing' (2 Sam 24:24).

To summarize what we have been discussing in this chapter, it may be useful to look at an example of how some of these principles work out in practice.

Let us take, as an example, a young married couple with two children whose gross income each month totals £500. This includes the husband's salary, plus Family Allowance and a small amount of income the wife earns as a helper in the local playgroup. After praying and talking matters over together they are agreed that their giving needs to be £75 each month. This is beyond the tithe (which would be £50) and is going to involve no little sacrifice on their part to balance the budget each month. But they are both convinced that God is calling them to step out in faith and prove his ability to meet all their needs. The £75 is set aside every month; £50 (the tithe) is apportioned to the local church. They have taken out a Deed of Covenant undertaking to pay to their local fellowship £600 per annum (twelve months × £50) and this means that the church treasurer can claim from the Inland Revenue an additional £257, making their total annual gift worth £857.

Of the £25 of the monthly gift remaining they send £10 each month to Tear Fund, for the support of a needy child in a Third World country. This helps to involve their own children in the discipline of Christian giving. Another £10 is given each month for the support of a missionary couple working among Muslims in the Middle East. The remaining £5 is committed to a Youth for Christ Schools worker who is based in a tough situation several hundred miles away, but they keep an active prayerful link in the work he is doing for the Lord. They simply cannot afford to have a 'special needs' fund, but on a regular basis they invite an unmarried mother in the church to come and share in a family meal and, when it is possible, they help her out in practical ways.

One small family, living in a semi in the suburbs, pressurized by a mortgage, growing kids and a demanding life. 'What can we do to advance the kingdom?' they might ask. Yet through their sacrificial giving and prayer the church in their town is able to reach out and minister to broken people; a child in Indonesia is helped to attend a Christian school where he will hear of the love of God as shown in Jesus; a young married couple can witness to Muslims and seek to build up new Christians in a hostile environment; school children in schools all over Blackburn will hear the gospel presented by a sincere young man with a burden to see disillusioned teenagers discover the freedom that Christ brings. And in their own neighbourhood, a wounded lady with a past she cannot forget but has to live with finds love, acceptance and an open home.

From the outside, 'No. 27' seems such an ordinary house. The casual observer would see nothing extraordinary in its occupants. But in terms of kingdom economics, it is a powerhouse. The lives of this little family touch the world. Their giving makes them builders of the kingdom.

7

Like a Mighty Army

For many years the Western world has been pre-occupied with the issue of prosperity. At such a time when the emphasis is on 'getting' one would imagine that the church would have much to say about 'giving'. Tragically our voice as Christians goes unheeded because our actions speak louder than our words. Instead of being 'an animated question mark', as someone has accurately described the task of the church, we have sold out to the ways of the world.

The revolution in our attitudes towards giving needs to begin with the individual but it must not rest there. The local church, as an expression of the body of Christ, needs radically to rethink its policies on how we use what God has entrusted to us.

Bishop Michael Baughen has written about his own experience as the leader of a local church facing the challenge of giving (Michael Baughen, *Moses and the Venture of Faith*, Mowbray). He writes of his personal commitment to the 'Moses principle' which led a hundred or so members in a Manchester parish to raise—by direct giving alone—almost £250 a head for a building project. Again under his leadership at

All Souls Church, London, the membership moved forward in faith as members gave £500 per person for an ambitious development scheme. In his book he quotes the road sign in the Australian outback that reads: 'Choose your rut carefully, you'll be in it for the next thirty miles!' All too often, that can be applied to churches that have not moved forward with God. At the present time, much is being written and discussed about change in structures and principles concerning church growth but it is one thing to change structures and something far deeper to change hearts. New wineskins are needed, but without the new wine to fill them they are useless.

An examination of churches in Britain that are growing under God's hand reveals certain key principles that are held in common. One of these principles stands out—growing churches *give*, and giving churches *grow*.

David Watson, a leader who has experienced first-hand rapid spiritual growth in the local church, has commented:

> Giving is usually a good sign of the spiritual state of any church. Most people are unable to give more generously until there is a deep work of the Holy Spirit releasing them from the desire to possess, which is so common to us all. Giving is a mark of God's Grace, and until people really know the Lord, are filled with His Love, there is unlikely to be much generous giving—except in one or two rare cases. (From a personal letter to the author. Used by permission.)

It is the work of the Holy Spirit to release us from the desire to possess, but how can we help that process?

How can leaders take their churches forward in faith and vision? What are our responsibilities as members to pray and work towards becoming living communities of faith that are moving with God on the question of giving? In short, how do we get out of the rut?

'Full of faith and of the Holy Spirit'

Spiritual revolution, if it is going to have a marked and lasting impact on a local church, must affect the leadership. 'You can never take people further than you have gone yourself' is an important maxim. In order to impart faith and vision to others, leaders must be men of faith and vision themselves.

We read in Acts that part of the missionary strategy of the early church was to appoint elders (or 'overseers') in each local church that had been established (Acts 14:23). Paul later writes to his colleague Timothy about the qualities that need to be seen in a man appointed to the ministry of eldership (1 Tim 3:1–7). They were to be godly men in every way. Similarly, deacons (or 'servants') were to be chosen on the basis of their Christ-like character that had won the respect of their fellow believers (1 Tim 3:8–13). Leadership in the early church was a serious business. Positions of power in the church were not for the status-seekers but for those in whose lives God was obviously at work. When a practical problem arose in the Jerusalem church over the daily distribution of food, the apostles instructed the church to choose men who could supervise the whole operation fairly. They were told to choose men: 'Who are known to be full of the Spirit and wisdom' (Acts 6:3). Luke gives us a list of the seven men who were chosen to carry out this duty. One of them, Stephen, is described as: 'a man full of faith and of the Holy Spirit' (Acts 6:5). When it came to the seemingly menial duty of looking after food distribution, the early Christians looked for men with *character* and *faith*.

We need leaders of quality in these dimensions. Sadly, it is possible for a man to be ordained for the task of leading the people of God, holding degrees and denominational political experience, but knowing little of the power of God. But, however a local church is led—whether by a group of elders, deacons, parish church council, or church committee—the quality of the leadership is of paramount importance; and that applies to full-time and lay leadership alike.

Too often people are chosen on the basis of seniority or sentiment. A person can be chosen for an office of influence because they are considered safe and respectable. Of course qualities such as integrity and stability are important, but whatever happened to 'men full of faith and of the Holy Spirit'? I am not advocating hot-headed extremism, but if a church is to move forward in faith and vision we need grenadiers not just guardians!

Leaders who hold the purse strings often clutch them too tightly. Some see themselves as celestial civil servants, charged with keeping the cash under lock and key, while doing their best to keep the corrupting rust and moth at bay. There is something seriously wrong with a 'community of faith' that hoards and holds money as if it was the most important thing in life.

John White, in his prophetic book *The Golden Cow* (Marshall, Morgan & Scott), tackles the issue of materialism in the twentieth-century church. He writes of Christians practising 'double insurance'. He points out that some churches keep large sums of money on deposit 'for a rainy day', to deal with emergencies such as the church roof falling in. In addition, members of such churches have their own savings prudently put on one side for the future. As John White points out, if disaster struck the church building then the members themselves could meet the need from their own resources or, if this was beyond their means, they could seek God! To hold money, *God's* money, in a bank while the world suffers for lack of bread (both spiritual and physical) is a blatant denial of the gospel we preach. Elsewhere in his book he highlights an important biblical principle:

> We must be suspicious of any faith about personal justification that is not substantiated by faith in God's power over material things in our everyday life. Faith about pie in the sky when I die cannot be demonstrated. Faith that God can supply my need today *can* be demonstrated. And if someone claims to possess justifying faith but shows no evidence of it, we may ask such a person whether he or she understands the difference between faith and mental assent. *Enslavement to the visible makes faith in the invisible suspect* (pp.41–2).

We would do well to re-read the parable of the talents (Mt 25:14–30) in the context of good stewardship. The whole basis of the master's judgement of his servants is how they *used* what was entrusted to them. The wicked, lazy servant was rebuked for not even using a deposit account to earn some interest on his master's money (at least most local churches have got that far!). But the central truth for us is that we are to *use* what God gives us. Hiding the money may have kept it safe, but the master's intention was more than security; he wanted to see it used wisely and well.

A local church can be paralysed for generations by a lack of spiritual vision. We need to pray for leaders 'full of faith and of the Holy Spirit'. Perhaps we are tempted to think that once spiritual renewal has come to a church then the giving will be more generous. In fact, I believe giving is one of the keys to bringing about spiritual renewal for a local fellowship. When the people of God begin to demonstrate that they mean business when they pray for revival—God acts. If we take Malachi's message seriously then we will be anxious to get our giving right, in order that the floodgates of God's blessing might be opened (Mal 2:10).

Responsible leadership

It is all very well to talk of the need for leaders with faith and vision, but what does this mean in practical terms? What are the responsibilities that leaders need to face to create a giving church?

Teaching and training

We cannot expect people to stumble over what the Bible teaches about giving. There must be clear, biblical teaching about giving. We need to 'tell it like it is', without fear or embarrassment. If we believe that sacrificial giving is part of Christian discipleship, then it needs to be taught in a clear, practical way. We must avoid the dangerous temptation of appealing for money only for a special project. This causes confusion, as people gain the impression that it is the particular need that is so important, rather than the principle of regular giving.

There is no substitute for clear Bible teaching, given by leaders who are sensitive to the needs of the people that they lead. Sensitivity to people's needs does not mean we avoid subjects that upset them, but rather we are made aware of the areas in which they must develop their faith.

Look at your church finances

As leaders we must take a long, hard look at what comes in and how we use it. If we are asking our members to give in a sacrificial way, are we setting them an example with the church budget? How much do we as a church actually give away? These are searching questions, but ones that need to be asked. I know of one church who faced this issue squarely and made a radical decision. They calculated the monthly 'housekeeping' needs of the church (i.e. what it cost to run the church). They laid this sum aside in the bank each month and gave the balance away—completely! They *chose* to live on a monthly basis in order to be reminded of their total dependence on God. The result of their decision was that money was released to meet many needs, both physical and spiritual, on a worldwide scale.

For some of us, as leaders, such a proposal may be breath-taking, but it is certainly heading in a New

Testament direction. We are called to be wise and responsible stewards, but we are also charged with the responsibility of leading people on in their faith in the invisible God. As always, example is the most exact teacher.

In my own church, following a period of teaching on the principles of giving, the leadership decided we needed an honest look at ourselves. I invited the fellowship to pray over the teaching they had received and then write expressing what they believed God was saying to us as a church family. The replies were not what we expected. We found greater faith and willingness among the people than some of us as leaders had. Here are some of the replies:

Together as a family we should be asking our Father what his will is and making this matter one of united prayer.

As a church we have a responsibility to others…our vision needs extending further, a commitment to people will surely yield a far greater response than vague financial requests for 'X' organization.

…the *sin* of affluence has much to answer for. Our young people expect a higher standard of living because they know no other way. We are all knowingly or unknowingly on the treadmill of a society which is seeking more and more at the expense of the 'have-nots' on the other side of the world…we feel as a church we should give more away…we need a call to commitment.

…for a while now I have been thinking 'Lord, as a church are we too rich?' Do we really need such a large bank balance…some may feel that we could use the minimum of our offering and give the rest away, then we would see God acting in a miraculous way.

I believe God is inviting us as a fellowship to use his resources. The only way we can do this is to have no resources of our own. While we have a bank balance of thousands we are hindered from his millions…. What right have we when men, women, children are dying of hunger…. Please don't let us continue to block up the flow of God's blessing by forcing it through a sprinkler!

Opening up the subject of giving in this way was both a challenge and a help to us as a leadership. Already we were 'tithing' our weekly offering with 10% going to mission, but God did not want us to sit back in self-satisfied ease. Not for the first time, the sheep were moving ahead of the shepherds.

Introspection is unhealthy but self-examination that leads to positive change is a vital ingredient for a growing church. Unlike the queen, in the story of Snow White, who wanted her mirror to say what she wanted to hear, we need to be prepared to look into the mirror of God's word with honesty—and expect honest answers!

A renewed commitment to mission

An inventor was showing a friend a new machine. It was an impressive sight. Flashing lights, wheels, cogs and pulleys—they all worked perfectly. 'Very nice,' the friend commented, 'but what does it actually *do*?' 'Well, it doesn't actually do anything,' the inventor replied, somewhat embarrassed, 'but doesn't it do it beautifully!'

What does the church actually *do*? What does it exist for? Such questions may seem obvious, but we need to make sure we are working on the basis of correct answers. Our programme may seem impressive but what are we aiming at?

As a leader in a local church I am of the conviction that there are two priorities that face us: *Fish* and *Fruit*. You may object at a seemingly naïve and even simplistic statement, but an examination of the New Testament reveals that the church is called first, to proclaim the kingdom of God and, secondly, to teach and encourage men and women to live lives of righteousness that are pleasing to God. The two are interwoven. In proclaiming the good news of the kingdom, we are to demonstrate the truth that we preach by the way that we live.

If we agree that the task of mission is a priority we must examine ourselves to see how much of our giving as a local church actually goes in that direction. Perhaps we find ourselves trapped into a pattern of giving that needs reviewing urgently. How informed are we about individuals and missions that we support? Instead of giving the 'usual' amount in the 'usual' direction, are we open to God leading us to do the *un*usual?

Mission is a big word, and I use it deliberately. We all, as local churches, need to be committed to the financial support of evangelism across the world. But we must not forget the material needs of the poor. In recent years there has been a new awakening of Christians to the plight of the poor. Christian relief agencies have shown a marked increase in giving and they badly need such support to minister the love of

Christ to a world in need. But there is almost a see-saw effect. Torn between evangelism and social action, we have often seen these issues as alternatives —an either/or situation. In fact it is a case of both/ and. As General William Booth, the founder of the Salvation Army, proved as he worked among the destitute in London's East End, people need the demonstration of the gospel as well as its message. 'Give a man some bread,' he said, 'but wrap it in a tract!'

A realistic evaluation of our church finances should lead us to examine our priorities in giving. If we take the great commission seriously then we must be prepared to make a renewed commitment to mission both in our prayers as well as by our gifts.

People before buildings

Howard Snyder, writing in his book *New Wine, New Wineskins* (Marshall, Morgan & Scott) speaks of the way in which our church buildings testify to our lack of flexibility and sometimes demonstrate our over-concern with lavish, ornate exteriors. But few of us would want to worship in a barn, and we realize how off-putting to the visitor peeling walls and an ice-cold church can be! As in all things, we need balance. It is God-honouring that the place where the church gathers to worship is in good condition and presents an atmosphere where people are not going to be distracted through discomfort. But, if we are honest, we spend more on buildings than we do on people.

Not far from my home there stands a church that has been running a fund-raising campaign to renovate the building. Outside there is an enormous billboard that reads 'Help Preserve This Ancient Church'. Every time I pass it, I shudder. There is something sadly wrong when the church goes, cap in hand, asking the world to bale them out of difficulty. The New Testament is clear: God does not have any holy buildings, only holy people. The church is people, not bricks and mortar. The building that we wrongly describe as 'the church', just happens to be the premises where *the* church meets together. If the building is crumbling around our ears or being an excessive drain on funds then we would do well to consider whether it is the best place for the church to meet.

'People matter more than things' is a thoroughly Christian ethic and one that needs to be incorporated in local church financial policy. Take, as an example of this, the issue of manpower. Many churches could increase their full-time leadership if they applied biblical principles on giving. Thankfully, we are moving away from the vision of the omnicompetent minister who, as the paid professional, is meant to be capable of fulfilling all the tasks of leadership. You do not need to be a vast church to have more than one leader set aside for full-time ministry. If ten earning members put their whole tithe into the church, it would create the financial support for an eleventh member to concentrate on the ministry that God has called them to do, without facing economic hardship. It could be that as a local church you have a concern for the young people in your community, perhaps many of them jobless and drifting. If God has raised up among you someone with obvious spiritual gifts who gets alongside young people, then it is within your reach as a congregation to release them into this valuable work. Obviously there are practical issues that must be faced concerning the person's call, gift, reliability and accountability—but the opportunities are before us, if we are willing to seize them.

I am a member of the pastoral team of a Baptist church in Essex. At the time of writing we have three full-time ministers, one full-time lady worker, and a part-time supplementary minister. As part of the church's commitment to world mission, I am released by the church to be involved in evangelism and teaching in various parts of the world. Our membership stands at around 300 people, none of whom are wealthy and the church does not have limitless resources in the bank. We have never been in a prosperous position to expand our team, but as the vision and work has increased we have been faced with the question, 'Is God calling us to take this step?' We have been tempted to ask the question, 'Can we afford it?', but it has seemed to us to be irrelevant. If God is telling someone to step out in faith, then he will meet the need. Throughout the development of our team ministry, God has provided enough for our needs. Our giving to mission and individuals with whom we have spiritual links has not diminished during this time, but rather it has significantly increased. I mention these things not as a matter of pride, but as a matter of fact. God provides when his people respond in faith.

Buildings do matter, but people are more important. A Christian-centred church is one where his love for people is reflected. If we spent as much time praying and seeking to help people as we do talking about the colour scheme for the church toilets, then society in Britain would be transformed.

Towards true fellowship

We have already seen that 'fellowship' for the New Testament church meant sharing at the deepest level. How do we create a church like that? The short answer is that we cannot—only God can create in his people the attitude of self-sacrifice. But we can pray and lead people towards that goal.

Whatever you may think about their theology, the house-church movement in Britain that has emerged in recent years has shown a refreshing desire for New Testament-style fellowship. In all movements there have been cases of excess and imbalance, but their striving towards *real* fellowship in the local church has echoed the deep longings of multitudes of Christian people in our nation. Gerald Coates, a controversial leader of the movement, has witnessed the steady growth of his own fellowship in Cobham, Surrey. He writes:

> The issue of finance basically moved us from being a ramshackle outfit of fairly happy people to a body of men and women in which there was order, sacrifice and mutual support.... When a woman's house burnt down we were the first on the scene, taking up an offering to help her financially, giving her furniture and also collecting loads of children's clothes that were washed and ironed for her family. The social services were staggered because we had already done a job of work before they could get the 'red tape' type machinery rolling. (From a personal letter to the author. Used by permission.)

No doubt this is a story that has been repeated in other parts of the country in 'establishment' churches—but it is the exception rather than the rule. Perhaps the advent of the welfare state has conditioned us to think that the faceless 'they' will take care of such practical needs, but the church of Christ was never meant to be a mere extension department of the social services. If the spirit of our age is 'get' then the spirit of God's people must be 'give'. Leaders who are truly God's men will not bully the church into economic fellowship but rather, by all means, they will seek to lead people to be givers rather than getters.

Do as I do

We have all heard the saying 'Don't do as I do, but do as I say!', but, as leaders, we are called to practise as well as preach. If we want to see people giving sacrificially, and trusting God with their possessions, then we must set a proper example. Why should God's people give when they see money hoarded or invested in stocks and shares for a rainy day that never comes? (Yes, that *does* happen!) Leaders are, by definition, those who lead and that leadership is seen by our own example.

Some years ago I was invited to speak at the anniversary of a church in the South of England. A small, struggling Christian community with thirty members, they had a handful of wage-earners among their number. In faith, they had committed themselves to an ambitious building project, not for the sake of possessing an ornate building, but because their work with underprivileged members of their community (particularly the lonely and mentally ill) made them realize that they needed a functional base for their God-given work. They undertook a scheme costing £100,000 which the outside observer would have dismissed as laughably unrealistic. They pressed on in faith and God began to meet the financial needs as they arose. The anniversary was the occasion for the members of the fellowship to bring their thankoffering to the Lord and, although they were already stretched by their sacrificial giving, they responded with open-hearted generosity. The minister announced to the fellowship that the leaders had prayed as to how this thankoffering was to be used, and the decision was taken that the entire amount should be given to a neighbouring church who were engaged in a similar building project. It did not seem to concern them that this other church was larger and, in many senses, in a better financial position. What mattered was, they were obedient to all that the Lord was asking them to do. The leaders of that small church were men of faith, and by example they were teaching their people *how* to trust God. Their own project was soon completed, with all the financial needs being met. God blessed them in their lives, he added to their number and he touched others through their example. The story of that little church is not about a formula, but it is about *faith*.

Responsible membership

Church membership must be more than having your name on a piece of paper. It has to do with belonging, responsibility and commitment. If we believe our-selves to be the body of Christ then our commitment is not to an organization called 'The Church Ltd', but first, to the Lord Jesus Christ and second, to his people.

What is the role of the member in a church that is learning to give? How can we play our part in encouraging others in the body of Christ to take this journey of faith? A number of responsibilities are before us:

Be a giver

Jesus warned us of the danger of judging others while ignoring the contradictions in our own lives:

> Why do you look at the speck of sawdust in your brother's eye and pay no attention to the plank in your own eye? (Mt 7:3).

Our first responsibility is to make sure that we ourselves are givers. The life of a giver is marked by love, the service of others, the practising of hospitality and the willingness to do it all without recognition or reward. You are not necessarily a giver because of the amount that you give. It is a question of a whole attitude of mind.

Instead of allowing frustration to grip you when you feel surrounded by those lacking in faith and vision, determine to be the person that God wants *you* to be.

Be informed

It is possible for us to be totally ignorant as to how our church finances are administered. We have a responsibility to be informed about such things. It is not 'unspiritual' to be concerned about how we use our money as a local church. Far from it! Asking questions and making suggestions in a positive, loving way can open the door to new possibilities of faith. It is one thing to trust leaders with such responsibilities and quite another to wash our hands of the whole business because we cannot be bothered. How much do you as a church give to overseas mission? How much for the upkeep of buildings? How much does the church have lying in the bank unused, and how long has it been there? It is time to get our heads out of the sand.

Be involved

Churches vary in the way they are governed, and in some there is more opportunity for members to be involved than in others. But, so far as we are able, we are called to involvement. We need to pray over the selection of elders/deacons/officers/parish church councils—whatever form the leadership may take. We need to look for the leadership qualities we have already discussed in this chapter. We must pray regularly for those in leadership to have ears that are open to God's voice. Where opportunities are given to discuss openly financial policies we must be prepared to get involved. God may call us to be involved in becoming leaders ourselves, and we need to be willing for such a possibility.

It could be that you are in a local church that supports outside agencies with which you are unhappy. Perhaps you feel that the money the church receives is squandered or, on the other hand, not used. Faced with these issues, it may be a case of 'To give or not to give? That is the question!' Should we continue to give to our local church when we are unhappy about how the money is used?

The first and most important question to answer is 'Am I in the right church?' If the answer is a clear 'yes', then it follows that you have a duty to give freely and sacrificially for the support of that work. The leadership of the local church are accountable to God for their stewardship. If we are unhappy about their stewardship we have a duty to pray and then share that concern with them. Again, it is the attitude of heart that counts. If we make our approach in an arrogant spirit we will antagonize and alienate. But if we go to them recognizing their authority and with a right attitude it will remind them that they 'are men who must give an account' (Heb 13:17).

As leaders and members, we each have our part to play in demonstrating the truth of the gospel by the way that we give. The needs and opportunities that face us today are staggering. Giving is *not* just another subject of Christian discipleship that we can index between 'A Happy Family Life' and 'How to Overcome Depression'. Giving tells us and—most important of all—it tells God, what we really feel about the King and his kingdom.

If we feel challenged then we must act—but time is running out . . . .

*   *   *

There is a battle raging. Broken bodies and torn limbs lie all around. The sounds of clashing steel and roaring cannon fill the air. The army is scattered, some have fled, tearing off their uniforms as they ran, to escape capture by the Enemy. Those who stand and fight are distanced. They fight only in small groups, each almost unaware of the others, because in war only generals see the field plan—for the fighting soldier it is hand-to-hand survival.

The Battle is fierce but the scattered army is not losing, although everything suggests it should be. Suddenly, the loud, clear blast of a trumpet is heard across the field. The fighting stops. Heads turn to see him as he rides upon his horse. His majesty is so apparent, his sovereignty so certain. Troops rush to his side from every direction, their mouths filled with cries and cheers. Slowly he begins to move forward with his cluster of fighters. The last battle is about to begin, and in their hearts the moving army finds an unmistakable sense of victory. They steel themselves, as soldiers do, for all that lies ahead. And each one silently remembers his vow of allegiance when first he marched behind the flag—*Everything belongs to him*.

*   *   *

Show me a kingdom where righteous men meet,
Show me a highway that is straight for their feet,
And I'll show you a place where God's all in all,
The Spirit is reigning for they've answered his call.

Show me a brother in whom self has no part,
Show me a sister who is pure in her heart,
And I'll show you a person to whom God's all in all,
The Spirit is reigning for they've answered his call.

Show me a family where sons are at peace,
Show me a home in which love will increase,
And I'll show you a dwelling where God's all in all,
The Spirit is reigning for they've answered his call.

Show me a church that has learned how to give,
Show me a people who know how to live,
And I'll show you a bride to whom God's all in all,
The Spirit is reigning for they've answered his call.

Also in paperback from Kingsway...

'Lord, let me give you a million dollars'

---

by Duane Logsdon *with Dan Wooding*

'Lord, if you really want me to give up my church pastorate and go full time into business, please let me, in return, give you back a million dollars.'

Duane had always been able to earn a living. But when he and his wife became Christians, a Bible college training launched him into a breadline ministry of pastoring new churches. As his family grew and his income withered, Duane and his wife teetered on the brink of nervous exhaustion and marital collapse.

A hard decision confronted them. Was the pastorate the only form of 'God's work'; or was there an alternative that would not threaten their precious family life?

Then Duane met Luis Palau, and the Lord opened up a new and unexpected avenue of service that would be a blessing to thousands all over the world.

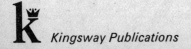

Kingsway Publications

What Shall It Profit...?

A look at some current economic issues with a Christian perspective

by Simon Webley

Do we really think inflation is an evil? Is there any answer to the frightening problem of mass unemployment? And what can *I* do to help the starving millions in other parts of the world?

Questions like these nag all of us from time to time. Christians in particular cannot simply shut their eyes and hope it will all go away. We should be familiar with the Bible's outlook on economic life; but we also need to understand the economic system and its effects on people's behaviour. This book has been written to help us on both counts, so that in an age of gloom and anxiety we can speak, pray and act with confidence and authority.

Simon Webley is Director of the British-North American Research Association and Chairman of TEAR Fund. He is married with three children.

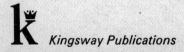

Kingsway Publications

Out of This World
Worldliness and the Christian

by John F. Balchin

'You are not of the world, but I chose you out of the world; therefore the world hates you' (John 15:19).

When God decided to make a people for himself, he could have removed them from the pressures of this world. But he didn't. Instead he called his people to a life that would glorify him right in the rough and tumble of everyday life and work. And he makes the same call today.

This book encourages Christians to live lives honouring to God in the midst of all that the twentieth century has to offer by way of false morality, materialism and a self-centred lifestyle. It challenges the church to avoid friendship with the world, while showing that Christians can remain involved in society as 'a colony of heaven on earth'.

Kingsway Publications

Rise Up and Build

by Nick Cuthbert

How near are we to a revival in Britain today?

Can God's people move on without restoration?

What has been achieved so far by the renewal movement?

The church in Britain has entered an era that is both exciting and challenging. Christians in 'house churches' and in the traditional denominations have come into new experiences of great personal blessing.

But what are we *building?*

Nick Cuthbert brings a word of encouragement and a word of warning. He calls on churches that are weary through failure—and those trapped by yesterday's blessings—to listen to what the Spirit is saying to the churches . . . and then obey.

If we want the church to be an effective force in our land, let's respond to God's call today.

Nick Cuthbert is a founder of the Jesus Centre in Birmingham. He is fully engaged in an evangelistic and teaching ministry.

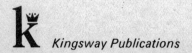

Kingsway Publications